The Essential Pottery Notebook

The Secret to Successful Kiln Firings

Kara Leigh Ford
Author of *Pottery for Beginners*

This book has been checked and endorsed by
The Edward Orton Foundation.

PAGE STREET
PUBLISHING CO.

PAGE STREET
PUBLISHING CO.

First published in 2025 by
Page Street Publishing Co.
27 Congress Street, Suite 1511
Salem, MA 01970
www.pagestreetpublishing.com

Distributed by Macmillan, sales in Canada by The Canadian Manda Group.

29 28 27 26 25 1 2 3 4 5

ISBN-13: 979-8-89003-2-003

Library of Congress Control Number: 2024933704

Edited by Alexandra Murphy
Cover and book design by Emma Hardy for Page Street Publishing Co.
Photography by Kara Leigh Ford and Dan Rushworth @quietinthewildphotography
This book has been checked and endorsed by The Edward Orton Foundation

Printed and bound in China

**I am dedicating this book to all the potters–
what a beautiful community we are.**

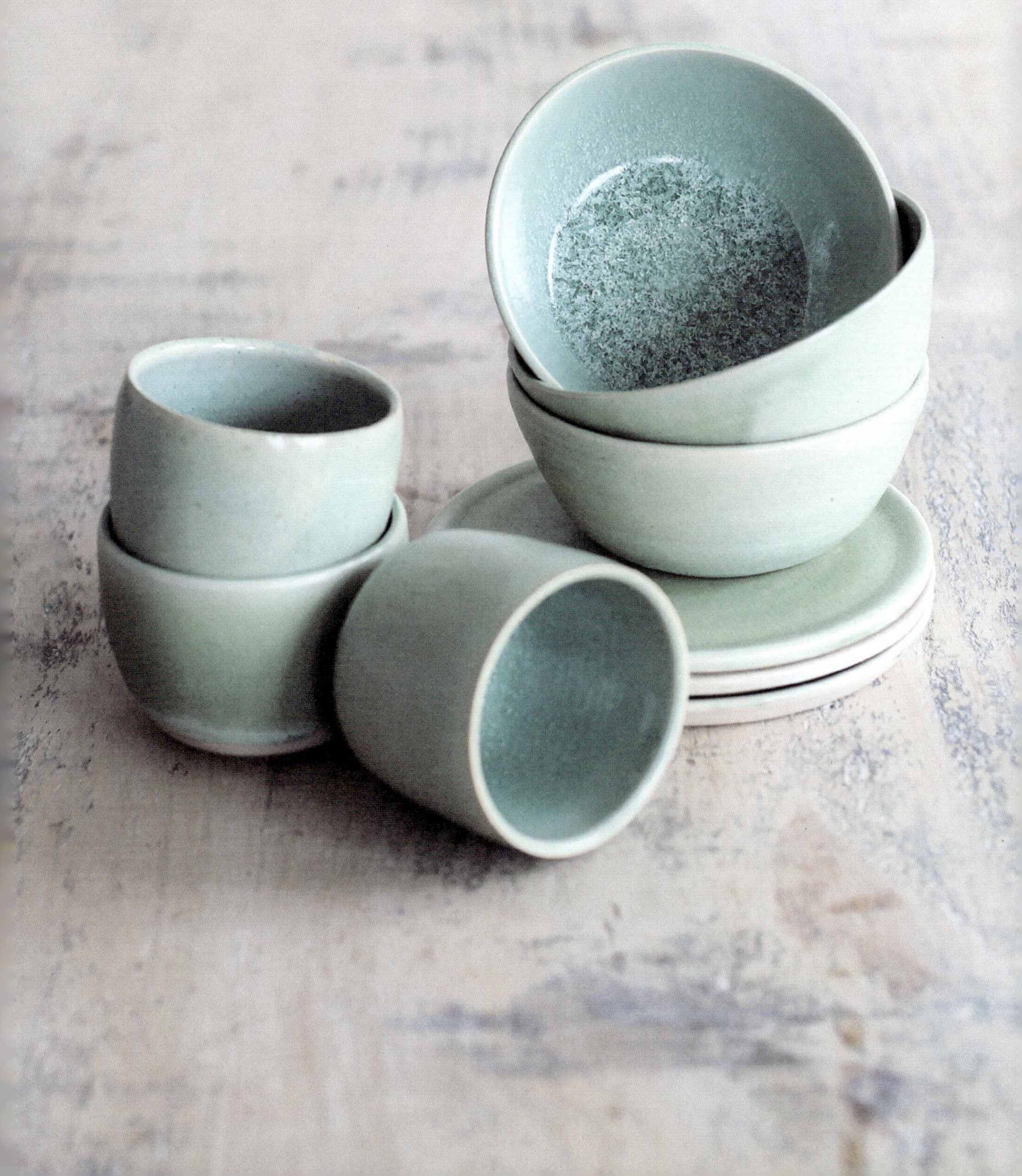

Contents

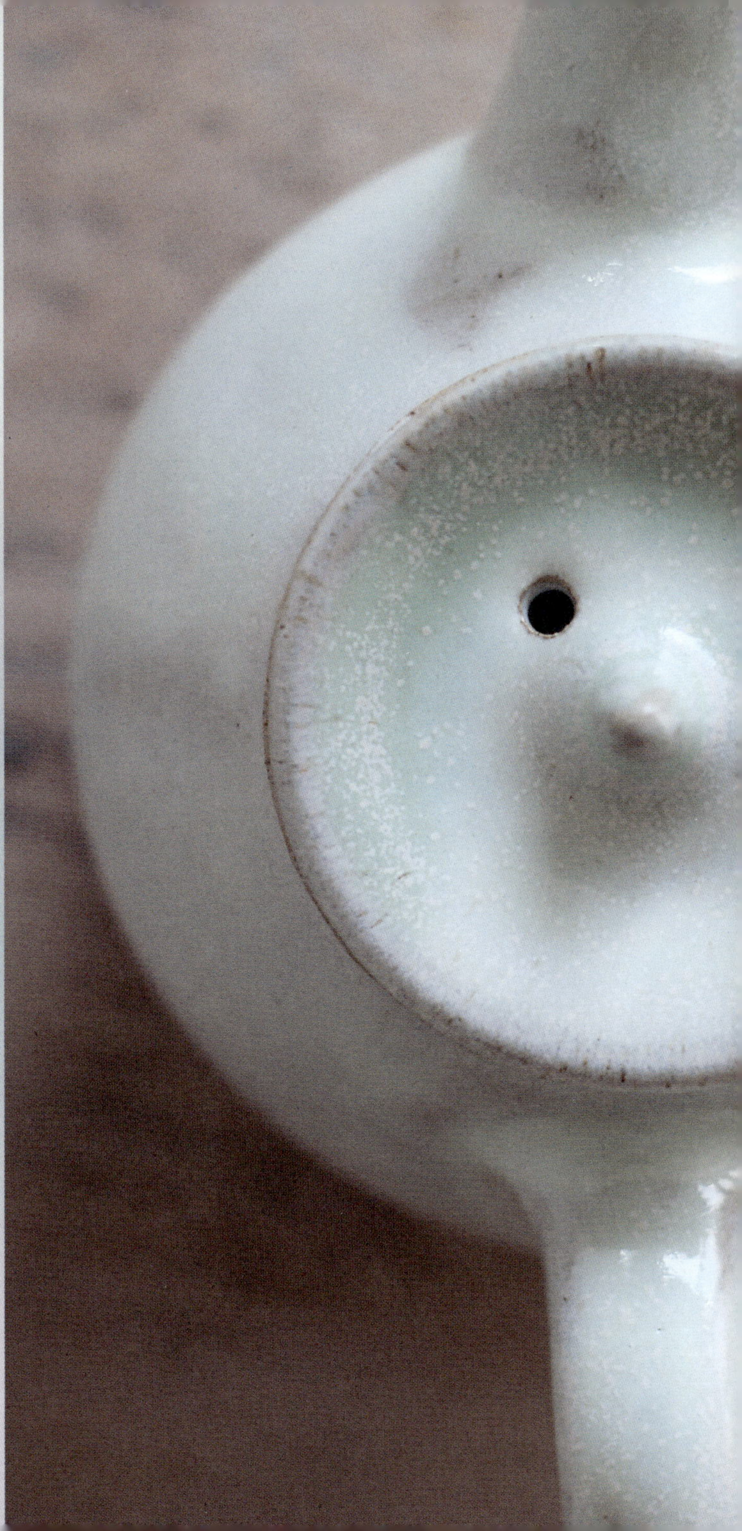

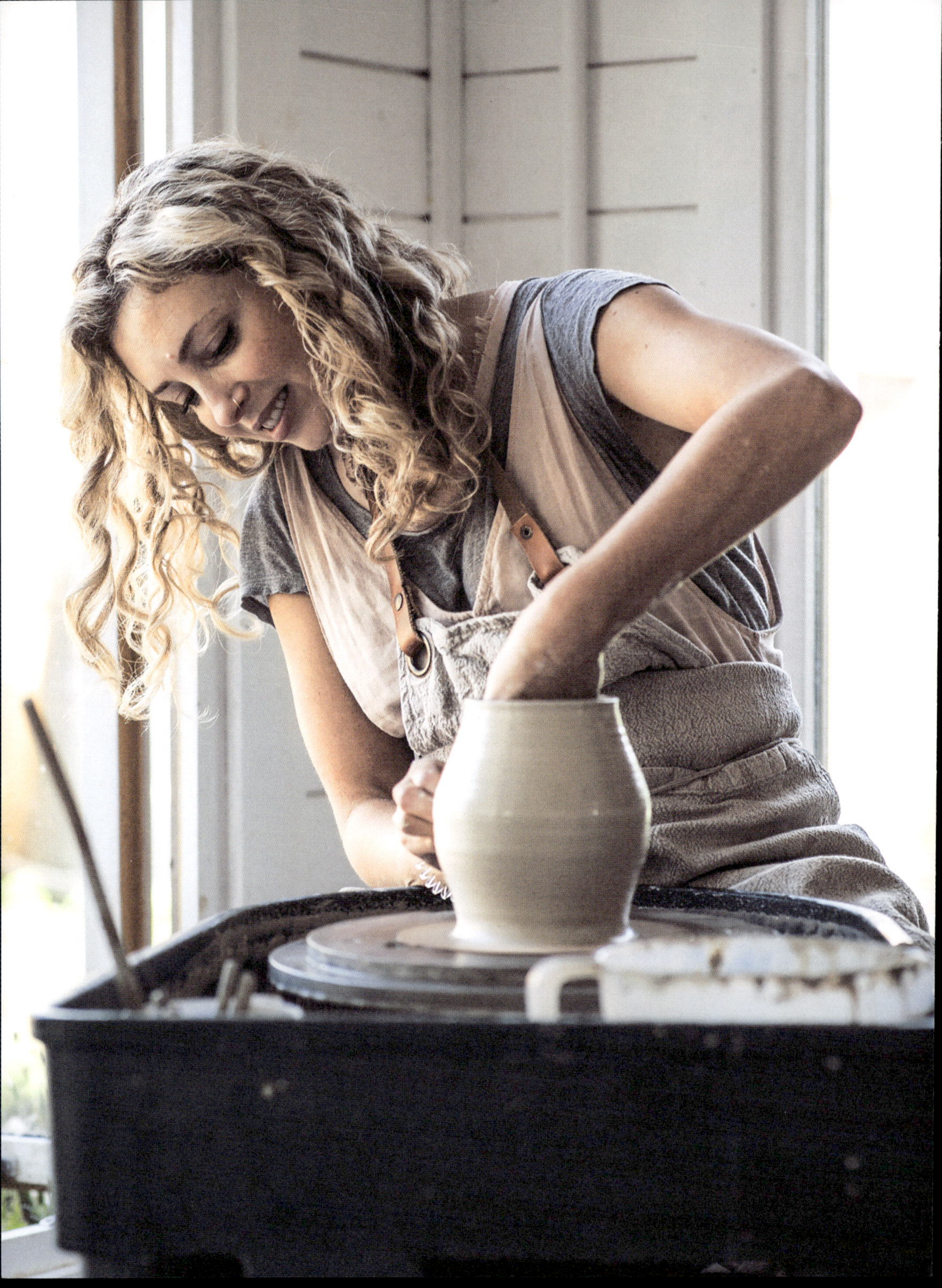

Introduction

Hello, I'm Kara.

I've been making pottery for nearly 20 years, and at the time of writing this I've been a full-time potter for 9 years. That doesn't even seem possible, but it's true. I'm predominantly a self-taught potter. I've had my work stocked in Fortnum & Mason. I've made plates for a Michelin-starred restaurant. I've taught hundreds of people pottery via workshops both in person and online via my Pottery Club. And I'm the author of *Pottery for Beginners*.

A few years ago, I was searching for a good pottery notebook but couldn't find one, so I created my own. Here it is. This notebook began as a way of keeping notes of my own kiln firings. Originally it was just in digital format, but as time went on, I knew how much my fellow potters would benefit from this tool and how useful it would be to make it into a real-life book that you can hold in your hands. It has evolved to include a ton of information on how to make your firings more successful, as well as an area to record your making processes too.

This notebook is a companion tool for all your pottery adventures. Keeping a pottery notebook doesn't just help you get excellent, repeatable results; it's also a lovely way to look back at your skill progression. Treat it like an artist's sketchbook or diary with added useful data. I hope this will always be your go-to notebook and a place to keep your notes for reference and posterity.

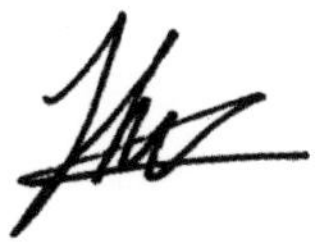

TIP FOR ELECTRIC KILN OWNERS

In this notebook there are 120 pages to record 120 firings. The average set of kiln elements lasts 100 firings. It's a great idea to start a new notebook when you get a new kiln or a new set of elements. When you're nearing the end of your notebook is when your elements might be wearing out and need changing. (Although this depends upon a few different factors, which I explain on page 169.)

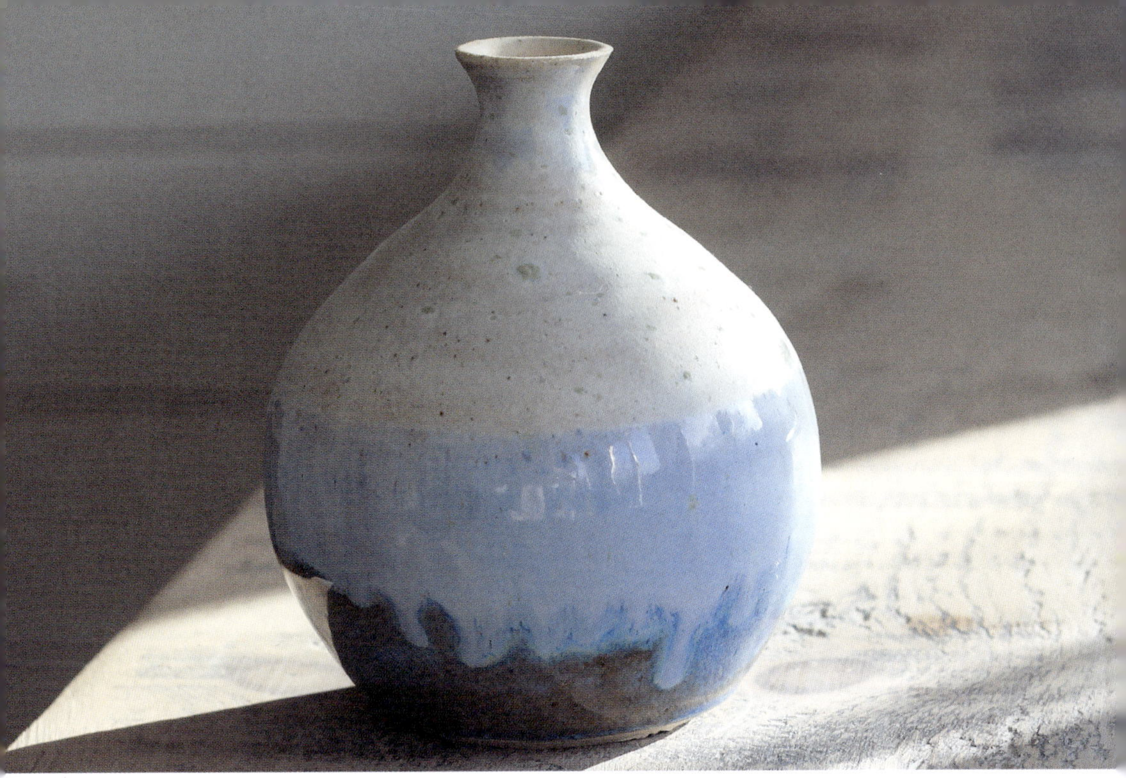

My Making Notes

This section is designed for you to keep sketches and notes of your designs. Your firing notes will follow. I have provided heaps of useful information in the final section at the back of the book, so do make sure you read that.

PRO TIPS

- Sketch out designs in clay as well as on paper. This will help you figure out if a design will work in 3D as well as in 2D. Gravity plays an important role in pottery!
- Keep a prototype of each design you are happy with. This will help you to replicate it in the future.

Calculating Shrinkage Rates

Everything you make will shrink approximately 10 to 20 percent on average from the wet raw clay to final firing. It's important to know how much. Most manufacturers list the shrinkage rate of the clay on their packaging, but you can also calculate it by making a shrinkage ruler.

Roll out a slab of your clay ¼ inch (0.6 cm) thick. Using a plastic ruler as a template, cut out two ruler shapes. Mark on them the inches or centimeters. Then leave them to dry. Pop one ruler in the glaze firing and one in the bisque. Then measure your fired rulers and compare them to the original to see the shrinkage rate of your clay at the different stages of making. **When recording the dimensions of your greenware, make sure you record whether it is freshly thrown, leather hard or bone dry.**

Formula

100% - [(Fired Ruler Length / Original Ruler Length) x 100]% = shrinkage percentage

Example

Original Ruler Length: 30 cm

Fired Ruler Length: 27 cm

27 / 30 = 0.9 x 100 = 90

Shrinkage rate = 100% – 90% = 10%

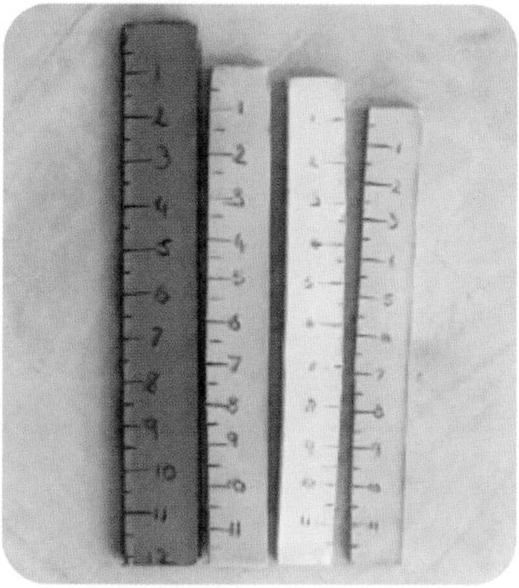

The longest, dark brown ruler on the far left shows the clay in its raw state—fresh out of the bag. The ruler next to it shows the clay in its bone dry or greenware state. The third ruler has been bisque fired. The ruler on the far right (though not glazed) has been fired to glazeware temperatures.

Making Notes

Dimensions

GREENWARE
(BEFORE FIRING)

Weight of clay used:

Height:

Width:

Depth:

FINISHED PIECE
(AFTER FIRING)

Height:

Width:

Depth:

Weight:

Shrinkage rate:

Dimensions

GREENWARE
(BEFORE FIRING)

Weight of clay used:

Height:

Width:

Depth:

FINISHED PIECE
(AFTER FIRING)

Height:

Width:

Depth:

Weight:

Shrinkage rate:

Making Notes

Dimensions

GREENWARE
(BEFORE FIRING)

Weight of clay used:

Height:

Width:

Depth:

FINISHED PIECE
(AFTER FIRING)

Height:

Width:

Depth:

Weight:

Shrinkage rate:

Dimensions

GREENWARE
(BEFORE FIRING)

Weight of clay used:

Height:

Width:

Depth:

FINISHED PIECE
(AFTER FIRING)

Height:

Width:

Depth:

Weight:

Shrinkage rate:

Making Notes

Dimensions

GREENWARE
(BEFORE FIRING)

Weight of clay used:

Height:

Width:

Depth:

FINISHED PIECE
(AFTER FIRING)

Height:

Width:

Depth:

Weight:

Shrinkage rate:

Dimensions

GREENWARE
(BEFORE FIRING)

Weight of clay used:

Height:

Width:

Depth:

FINISHED PIECE
(AFTER FIRING)

Height:

Width:

Depth:

Weight:

Shrinkage rate:

Making Notes

Dimensions

GREENWARE
(BEFORE FIRING)

Weight of clay used:

Height:

Width:

Depth:

FINISHED PIECE
(AFTER FIRING)

Height:

Width:

Depth:

Weight:

Shrinkage rate:

Dimensions

GREENWARE
(BEFORE FIRING)

Weight of clay used:

Height:

Width:

Depth:

FINISHED PIECE
(AFTER FIRING)

Height:

Width:

Depth:

Weight:

Shrinkage rate:

Making Notes

Dimensions

GREENWARE (BEFORE FIRING)

Weight of clay used:

Height:

Width:

Depth:

FINISHED PIECE (AFTER FIRING)

Height:

Width:

Depth:

Weight:

Shrinkage rate:

Dimensions

GREENWARE (BEFORE FIRING)

Weight of clay used:

Height:

Width:

Depth:

FINISHED PIECE (AFTER FIRING)

Height:

Width:

Depth:

Weight:

Shrinkage rate:

Making Notes

Dimensions

GREENWARE (BEFORE FIRING)

Weight of clay used:

Height:

Width:

Depth:

FINISHED PIECE (AFTER FIRING)

Height:

Width:

Depth:

Weight:

Shrinkage rate:

Dimensions

GREENWARE (BEFORE FIRING)

Weight of clay used:

Height:

Width:

Depth:

FINISHED PIECE (AFTER FIRING)

Height:

Width:

Depth:

Weight:

Shrinkage rate:

Making Notes

Dimensions

GREENWARE (BEFORE FIRING)

Weight of clay used:

Height:

Width:

Depth:

FINISHED PIECE (AFTER FIRING)

Height:

Width:

Depth:

Weight:

Shrinkage rate:

Dimensions

GREENWARE (BEFORE FIRING)

Weight of clay used:

Height:

Width:

Depth:

FINISHED PIECE (AFTER FIRING)

Height:

Width:

Depth:

Weight:

Shrinkage rate:

Making Notes

Dimensions

GREENWARE (BEFORE FIRING)

Weight of clay used:

Height:

Width:

Depth:

FINISHED PIECE (AFTER FIRING)

Height:

Width:

Depth:

Weight:

Shrinkage rate:

Dimensions

GREENWARE (BEFORE FIRING)

Weight of clay used:

Height:

Width:

Depth:

FINISHED PIECE (AFTER FIRING)

Height:

Width:

Depth:

Weight:

Shrinkage rate:

Making Notes

Dimensions

GREENWARE (BEFORE FIRING)

Weight of clay used:

Height:

Width:

Depth:

FINISHED PIECE (AFTER FIRING)

Height:

Width:

Depth:

Weight:

Shrinkage rate:

Dimensions

GREENWARE (BEFORE FIRING)

Weight of clay used:

Height:

Width:

Depth:

FINISHED PIECE (AFTER FIRING)

Height:

Width:

Depth:

Weight:

Shrinkage rate:

Making Notes

Dimensions

GREENWARE
(BEFORE FIRING)

Weight of clay used:

Height:

Width:

Depth:

FINISHED PIECE
(AFTER FIRING)

Height:

Width:

Depth:

Weight:

Shrinkage rate:

Dimensions

GREENWARE
(BEFORE FIRING)

Weight of clay used:

Height:

Width:

Depth:

FINISHED PIECE
(AFTER FIRING)

Height:

Width:

Depth:

Weight:

Shrinkage rate:

Making Notes

Dimensions

GREENWARE (BEFORE FIRING)

Weight of clay used:

Height:

Width:

Depth:

FINISHED PIECE (AFTER FIRING)

Height:

Width:

Depth:

Weight:

Shrinkage rate:

Dimensions

GREENWARE (BEFORE FIRING)

Weight of clay used:

Height:

Width:

Depth:

FINISHED PIECE (AFTER FIRING)

Height:

Width:

Depth:

Weight:

Shrinkage rate:

Making Notes

Dimensions

GREENWARE (BEFORE FIRING)

Weight of clay used:

Height:

Width:

Depth:

FINISHED PIECE (AFTER FIRING)

Height:

Width:

Depth:

Weight:

Shrinkage rate:

Dimensions

GREENWARE (BEFORE FIRING)

Weight of clay used:

Height:

Width:

Depth:

FINISHED PIECE (AFTER FIRING)

Height:

Width:

Depth:

Weight:

Shrinkage rate:

Making Notes

Dimensions

GREENWARE
(BEFORE FIRING)

Weight of clay used:

Height:

Width:

Depth:

FINISHED PIECE
(AFTER FIRING)

Height:

Width:

Depth:

Weight:

Shrinkage rate:

Dimensions

GREENWARE
(BEFORE FIRING)

Weight of clay used:

Height:

Width:

Depth:

FINISHED PIECE
(AFTER FIRING)

Height:

Width:

Depth:

Weight:

Shrinkage rate:

Making Notes

Dimensions

GREENWARE (BEFORE FIRING)

Weight of clay used:

Height:

Width:

Depth:

FINISHED PIECE (AFTER FIRING)

Height:

Width:

Depth:

Weight:

Shrinkage rate:

Dimensions

GREENWARE (BEFORE FIRING)

Weight of clay used:

Height:

Width:

Depth:

FINISHED PIECE (AFTER FIRING)

Height:

Width:

Depth:

Weight:

Shrinkage rate:

Making Notes

Dimensions

GREENWARE (BEFORE FIRING)

Weight of clay used:

Height:

Width:

Depth:

FINISHED PIECE (AFTER FIRING)

Height:

Width:

Depth:

Weight:

Shrinkage rate:

Dimensions

GREENWARE (BEFORE FIRING)

Weight of clay used:

Height:

Width:

Depth:

FINISHED PIECE (AFTER FIRING)

Height:

Width:

Depth:

Weight:

Shrinkage rate:

Making Notes

Dimensions

GREENWARE
(BEFORE FIRING)

Weight of clay used:

Height:

Width:

Depth:

FINISHED PIECE
(AFTER FIRING)

Height:

Width:

Depth:

Weight:

Shrinkage rate:

Dimensions

GREENWARE
(BEFORE FIRING)

Weight of clay used:

Height:

Width:

Depth:

FINISHED PIECE
(AFTER FIRING)

Height:

Width:

Depth:

Weight:

Shrinkage rate:

Making Notes

Dimensions

GREENWARE (BEFORE FIRING)

Weight of clay used:

Height:

Width:

Depth:

FINISHED PIECE (AFTER FIRING)

Height:

Width:

Depth:

Weight:

Shrinkage rate:

Dimensions

GREENWARE (BEFORE FIRING)

Weight of clay used:

Height:

Width:

Depth:

FINISHED PIECE (AFTER FIRING)

Height:

Width:

Depth:

Weight:

Shrinkage rate:

Making Notes

Dimensions

GREENWARE (BEFORE FIRING)

Weight of clay used:

Height:

Width:

Depth:

FINISHED PIECE (AFTER FIRING)

Height:

Width:

Depth:

Weight:

Shrinkage rate:

Dimensions

GREENWARE (BEFORE FIRING)

Weight of clay used:

Height:

Width:

Depth:

FINISHED PIECE (AFTER FIRING)

Height:

Width:

Depth:

Weight:

Shrinkage rate:

Making Notes

Dimensions

GREENWARE (BEFORE FIRING)

Weight of clay used:

Height:

Width:

Depth:

FINISHED PIECE (AFTER FIRING)

Height:

Width:

Depth:

Weight:

Shrinkage rate:

Dimensions

GREENWARE (BEFORE FIRING)

Weight of clay used:

Height:

Width:

Depth:

FINISHED PIECE (AFTER FIRING)

Height:

Width:

Depth:

Weight:

Shrinkage rate:

Making Notes

Dimensions

GREENWARE
(BEFORE FIRING)

Weight of clay used:

Height:

Width:

Depth:

FINISHED PIECE
(AFTER FIRING)

Height:

Width:

Depth:

Weight:

Shrinkage rate:

Dimensions

GREENWARE
(BEFORE FIRING)

Weight of clay used:

Height:

Width:

Depth:

FINISHED PIECE
(AFTER FIRING)

Height:

Width:

Depth:

Weight:

Shrinkage rate:

Making Notes

Dimensions

GREENWARE
(BEFORE FIRING)

Weight of clay used:

Height:

Width:

Depth:

FINISHED PIECE
(AFTER FIRING)

Height:

Width:

Depth:

Weight:

Shrinkage rate:

Dimensions

GREENWARE
(BEFORE FIRING)

Weight of clay used:

Height:

Width:

Depth:

FINISHED PIECE
(AFTER FIRING)

Height:

Width:

Depth:

Weight:

Shrinkage rate:

Making Notes

Dimensions

GREENWARE (BEFORE FIRING)

Weight of clay used:

Height:

Width:

Depth:

FINISHED PIECE (AFTER FIRING)

Height:

Width:

Depth:

Weight:

Shrinkage rate:

Dimensions

GREENWARE (BEFORE FIRING)

Weight of clay used:

Height:

Width:

Depth:

FINISHED PIECE (AFTER FIRING)

Height:

Width:

Depth:

Weight:

Shrinkage rate:

Making Notes

Dimensions

GREENWARE (BEFORE FIRING)

Weight of clay used:

Height:

Width:

Depth:

FINISHED PIECE (AFTER FIRING)

Height:

Width:

Depth:

Weight:

Shrinkage rate:

Dimensions

GREENWARE (BEFORE FIRING)

Weight of clay used:

Height:

Width:

Depth:

FINISHED PIECE (AFTER FIRING)

Height:

Width:

Depth:

Weight:

Shrinkage rate:

Making Notes

Dimensions

GREENWARE
(BEFORE FIRING)

Weight of clay used:

Height:

Width:

Depth:

FINISHED PIECE
(AFTER FIRING)

Height:

Width:

Depth:

Weight:

Shrinkage rate:

Dimensions

GREENWARE
(BEFORE FIRING)

Weight of clay used:

Height:

Width:

Depth:

FINISHED PIECE
(AFTER FIRING)

Height:

Width:

Depth:

Weight:

Shrinkage rate:

Making Notes

Dimensions

GREENWARE (BEFORE FIRING)

Weight of clay used:

Height:

Width:

Depth:

FINISHED PIECE (AFTER FIRING)

Height:

Width:

Depth:

Weight:

Shrinkage rate:

Dimensions

GREENWARE (BEFORE FIRING)

Weight of clay used:

Height:

Width:

Depth:

FINISHED PIECE (AFTER FIRING)

Height:

Width:

Depth:

Weight:

Shrinkage rate:

Making Notes

Dimensions

GREENWARE
(BEFORE FIRING)

Weight of clay used:

Height:

Width:

Depth:

FINISHED PIECE
(AFTER FIRING)

Height:

Width:

Depth:

Weight:

Shrinkage rate:

Dimensions

GREENWARE
(BEFORE FIRING)

Weight of clay used:

Height:

Width:

Depth:

FINISHED PIECE
(AFTER FIRING)

Height:

Width:

Depth:

Weight:

Shrinkage rate:

My Kiln Notes

Note: These kiln notes have been made predominantly for electric kiln firings but can be modified for gas reduction firings, raku firings, etc.

1. Check which option is relevant.
2. When did you do this firing?
3. This is how many firings the sets of elements have had (e.g., For new elements, write "1," and on the next firing write "2"). Even if you don't know how many firings they have done, this is still useful to note so you have a record of subsequent firings.
4. List the glazes and clay used in this firing. See page 38 for info on Specific Gravity.
5. See page 186 for info about schedules. Fahrenheit has been used in the example, but you can use Celsius if preferred.
6. (Optional) Slow cool helps to develop crystals in certain glazes. See page 189 for suggested slow cool schedule.
7. Use this section to record application info (e.g., dipping, pouring, brush on, etc.).
8. This does not include cooling time.
9. Not all kiln controllers give you this info. Check your kiln controller manual to see if this is applicable. **Note:** KW usage going up dramatically is a good indication that the elements might need changing soon.
10. Helps you keep track of your costs (which could inform your prices if you sell your work). For those who do not have a kiln controller which provides the KW usage, see the formula provided on page 39.
11. How you pack a kiln will affect the firing. See page 181 for details.
12. Perfect—I've never seen anything so beautiful—to Disaster. Don't worry, failures mean your next firing will be better.
13. Record the cone pack you use and the number of the cone(s) that bent correctly. In the example, a different cone pack was used on each shelf. See page 171 for information on cones.
14. Use this wherever extra space is needed, such as details of reduction firings, or to explain what happened with the glaze results.

Kiln Notes Firing Records

EXAMPLE

1 BISQUE ✓ GLAZE

2 DATE: July 29, 2024

OTHER:

3 FIRING NO.: 1

4 CLAY, GLAZES & RECIPES USED

satin white stoneware dipping glaze on Staffordshire stoneware

Specific Gravity: 1.45

5 SCHEDULE

Ramp 1: 210°F per hour to 570°F

Ramp 2: 300°F per hour to 2225°F

Ramp 3:

Ramp 4:

Soak: 15 minutes

6 Slow cool:

7 GLAZE TECHNIQUES

Double dip, 3-second dip

8 Length of firing hours: 10.5 hours

9 KW used: 57.1 KW

10 Cost: $20.75

11 PACK

Tight — Moderate ✓ — Loose

12 GLAZE RESULT

- Perfect
- Good ✓
- OK
- Could be better
- Disaster

- Underfired
- Bang on!
- Overfired ✓

Slightly overfired

13 CONES USED

5 6 7

CONE ACHIEVED

Top: 6

Middle: 7

Bottom: 6

14 ADDITIONAL INFO

What went wrong: the glazes on the middle shelf were runny. Maybe the kiln got too hot?

What went right: Colors were lovely.

Suggestions for next firing: slightly too much heat work. Reduce top temperature or remove the soak.

Calculating Specific Gravity

Measuring the specific gravity of your glaze is a way of checking you have the correct ratio of water to glaze material. This is especially relevant for dipping glazes and for those who make their own glazes from raw materials based on a recipe.

Specific gravity has to do with the "fit" of the glaze. Imagine the glaze is like clothing that the clay wears. If there is too much glaze material in the glaze, the clothing may become too tight. Put stress on the clay (such as pouring in hot water), and the clothing may tear. This can create faults in your pottery, such as a crack. Too little glaze material in the glaze and it may become too weak. This may make it very powdery before it's fired and chip easily. The color of the glaze may also come out wishy-washy or brown.

Most glazes work best between 1.4 and 1.6, but there are exceptions to this. Only by testing will you find the correct specific gravity of your glaze. You can measure specific gravity using a graduated cylinder and a digital scale. **Note:** Make sure you stir the glaze really well before measuring.

Specific Gravity Formula

Weight in grams of glaze / Volume in ml of the glaze

Example

700 grams / 500 ml = 1.4

Keeping the specific gravity of your glaze consistent at a ratio you know works well will help you to reproduce good glaze results.

- If your specific gravity is too high, you need to add water. Do this gradually, recalculating the gravity in between.
- If your specific gravity is too low, you can add more glaze material or you can allow the glaze to settle overnight and syphon off some of the water.

Calculating Cost of Firings

If your kiln controller does not give you information on KW usage or cost, here's a formula to help you! You'll need the following information:

- Cost of electricity per kilowatt hour (kWh) – These vary from location to location, so make sure to look up your local electricity tariff.
- Kilowatt rating of the kiln – This is normally written on a metal panel on the side of the kiln.
- Program duration in hours.
- Duty cycle of the kiln – The elements are not on for the entire firing cycle. A duty cycle of the kiln is the amount of time electricity is actually passing through the elements, when the relays are turned on. You will hear when the relays turn on and off by the clicks. A duty cycle is typically 60%. You would express this value as a decimal, e.g., 0.6.

Formula

(Cost of electricity per kilowatt hour) x (kilowatt rating of the kiln) x (program duration in hours) x (duty cycle of the kiln)

Example

$0.35 x 7.5 x 8 hours x 0.6 = $12.60

PRO TIP

Take photos of your pots and put them into a digital folder labeled with the corresponding number of your firing and the date. It's a great idea to take a photo of your cones too so you can have a visual reference of the heat work without needing to keep all your cones.

Kiln Notes
Firing Records

BISQUE GLAZE DATE: ____________

OTHER: ____________ FIRING NO.: ____________

CLAY, GLAZES & RECIPES USED

Specific Gravity:

GLAZE TECHNIQUES

SCHEDULE

Ramp 1:

Ramp 2:

Ramp 3:

Ramp 4:

Soak:

Slow cool:

Length of firing hours:

KW used:

Cost:

PACK

Tight Moderate Loose

CONES USED

CONE ACHIEVED

GLAZE RESULT

Perfect

Good

OK

Could be better

Disaster

Underfired

Bang on!

Overfired

ADDITIONAL INFO

What went wrong:

What went right:

Suggestions for next firing:

Kiln Notes Firing Records

BISQUE GLAZE DATE: ____________

OTHER: ____________ FIRING NO.: ____________

CLAY, GLAZES & RECIPES USED

Specific Gravity:

GLAZE TECHNIQUES

SCHEDULE

Ramp 1:

Ramp 2:

Ramp 3:

Ramp 4:

Soak:

Slow cool:

Length of firing hours:

KW used:

Cost:

PACK

Tight Moderate Loose

CONES USED

CONE ACHIEVED

GLAZE RESULT

- Perfect
- Good
- OK
- Could be better
- Disaster

- Underfired
- Bang on!
- Overfired

ADDITIONAL INFO

What went wrong:

What went right:

Suggestions for next firing:

Kiln Notes
Firing Records

BISQUE   GLAZE   DATE: ______

OTHER: ______   FIRING NO.: ______

CLAY, GLAZES & RECIPES USED

Specific Gravity:

SCHEDULE

Ramp 1:

Ramp 2:

Ramp 3:

Ramp 4:

Soak:

Slow cool:

Length of firing hours:

KW used:

Cost:

GLAZE TECHNIQUES

PACK

Tight   Moderate   Loose

CONES USED

CONE ACHIEVED

GLAZE RESULT

Perfect

Good

OK

Could be better

Disaster

Underfired

Bang on!

Overfired

ADDITIONAL INFO

What went wrong:

What went right:

Suggestions for next firing:

Kiln Notes Firing Records

BISQUE GLAZE DATE: ____________

OTHER: ____________ FIRING NO.: ____________

CLAY, GLAZES & RECIPES USED

Specific Gravity:

GLAZE TECHNIQUES

SCHEDULE

Ramp 1:

Ramp 2:

Ramp 3:

Ramp 4:

Soak:

Slow cool:

Length of firing hours:

KW used:

Cost:

PACK

Tight Moderate Loose

CONES USED

CONE ACHIEVED

GLAZE RESULT

Perfect

Good

OK

Could be better

Disaster

Underfired

Bang on!

Overfired

ADDITIONAL INFO

What went wrong:

What went right:

Suggestions for next firing:

Kiln Notes
Firing Records

BISQUE   GLAZE   DATE: ______

OTHER: ______   FIRING NO.: ______

CLAY, GLAZES & RECIPES USED

Specific Gravity:

SCHEDULE

Ramp 1:

Ramp 2:

Ramp 3:

Ramp 4:

Soak:

Slow cool:

GLAZE TECHNIQUES

Length of firing hours:

KW used:

Cost:

PACK

Tight   Moderate   Loose

GLAZE RESULT

Perfect   Underfired

Good   Bang on!

OK   Overfired

Could be better

Disaster

CONES USED

CONE ACHIEVED

ADDITIONAL INFO

What went wrong: What went right: Suggestions for next firing:

Kiln Notes Firing Records

○ BISQUE ○ GLAZE DATE: ______

○ OTHER: ______ FIRING NO.: ______

CLAY, GLAZES & RECIPES USED

Specific Gravity:

SCHEDULE

Ramp 1:

Ramp 2:

Ramp 3:

Ramp 4:

Soak:

Slow cool:

GLAZE TECHNIQUES

Length of firing hours:

KW used:

Cost:

PACK

Tight — Moderate — Loose

GLAZE RESULT

○ Perfect
○ Good
○ OK
○ Could be better
○ Disaster

○ Underfired
○ Bang on!
○ Overfired

CONES USED

CONE ACHIEVED

ADDITIONAL INFO

What went wrong:

What went right:

Suggestions for next firing:

Kiln Notes
Firing Records

BISQUE GLAZE DATE:

OTHER: FIRING NO.:

CLAY, GLAZES & RECIPES USED

Specific Gravity:

SCHEDULE

Ramp 1:

Ramp 2:

Ramp 3:

Ramp 4:

Soak:

Slow cool:

GLAZE TECHNIQUES

Length of firing hours:

KW used:

Cost:

PACK

Tight Moderate Loose

CONES USED CONE ACHIEVED

GLAZE RESULT

Perfect Underfired

Good Bang on!

OK Overfired

Could be better

Disaster

ADDITIONAL INFO

What went wrong: What went right: Suggestions for next firing:

Kiln Notes
Firing Records

BISQUE   GLAZE   DATE: ______

OTHER: ______   FIRING NO.: ______

CLAY, GLAZES & RECIPES USED

Specific Gravity:

GLAZE TECHNIQUES

SCHEDULE

Ramp 1:

Ramp 2:

Ramp 3:

Ramp 4:

Soak:

Slow cool:

Length of firing hours:

KW used:

Cost:

PACK

Tight   Moderate   Loose

CONES USED

CONE ACHIEVED

GLAZE RESULT

Perfect

Good

OK

Could be better

Disaster

Underfired

Bang on!

Overfired

ADDITIONAL INFO

What went wrong:

What went right:

Suggestions for next firing:

Kiln Notes
Firing Records

BISQUE GLAZE DATE: ______

OTHER: ______ FIRING NO.: ______

CLAY, GLAZES & RECIPES USED

Specific Gravity:

SCHEDULE

Ramp 1:

Ramp 2:

Ramp 3:

Ramp 4:

Soak:

Slow cool:

GLAZE TECHNIQUES

Length of firing hours:

KW used:

Cost:

PACK

Tight Moderate Loose

CONES USED CONE ACHIEVED

GLAZE RESULT

Perfect
Good
OK
Could be better
Disaster

Underfired
Bang on!
Overfired

ADDITIONAL INFO

What went wrong:

What went right:

Suggestions for next firing:

Kiln Notes Firing Records

BISQUE GLAZE DATE: ____________

OTHER: ____________ FIRING NO.: ____________

CLAY, GLAZES & RECIPES USED

Specific Gravity:

SCHEDULE

Ramp 1:

Ramp 2:

Ramp 3:

Ramp 4:

Soak:

Slow cool:

Length of firing hours:

KW used:

Cost:

GLAZE TECHNIQUES

PACK

Tight Moderate Loose

CONES USED

CONE ACHIEVED

GLAZE RESULT

- Perfect
- Good
- OK
- Could be better
- Disaster

- Underfired
- Bang on!
- Overfired

ADDITIONAL INFO

What went wrong:

What went right:

Suggestions for next firing:

Kiln Notes Firing Records

BISQUE GLAZE DATE:

OTHER: FIRING NO.:

CLAY, GLAZES & RECIPES USED

Specific Gravity:

SCHEDULE

Ramp 1:

Ramp 2:

Ramp 3:

Ramp 4:

Soak:

Slow cool:

Length of firing hours:

KW used:

Cost:

GLAZE TECHNIQUES

PACK

Tight Moderate Loose

CONES USED

CONE ACHIEVED

GLAZE RESULT

Perfect

Good

OK

Could be better

Disaster

Underfired

Bang on!

Overfired

ADDITIONAL INFO

What went wrong:

What went right:

Suggestions for next firing:

Kiln Notes
Firing Records

BISQUE GLAZE DATE: ______________

OTHER: ______________ FIRING NO.: ______________

CLAY, GLAZES & RECIPES USED

Specific Gravity:

SCHEDULE

Ramp 1:

Ramp 2:

Ramp 3:

Ramp 4:

Soak:

Slow cool:

Length of firing hours:

KW used:

Cost:

GLAZE TECHNIQUES

PACK

Tight — Moderate — Loose

GLAZE RESULT

- Perfect
- Good
- OK
- Could be better
- Disaster

- Underfired
- Bang on!
- Overfired

CONES USED

CONE ACHIEVED

ADDITIONAL INFO

What went wrong:

What went right:

Suggestions for next firing:

Kiln Notes
Firing Records

BISQUE GLAZE DATE: ____________

OTHER: ____________ FIRING NO.: ____________

CLAY, GLAZES & RECIPES USED

Specific Gravity:

GLAZE TECHNIQUES

SCHEDULE

Ramp 1:

Ramp 2:

Ramp 3:

Ramp 4:

Soak:

Slow cool:

Length of firing hours:

KW used:

Cost:

PACK

Tight Moderate Loose

CONES USED CONE ACHIEVED

GLAZE RESULT

Perfect

Good

OK

Could be better

Disaster

Underfired

Bang on!

Overfired

ADDITIONAL INFO

What went wrong:

What went right:

Suggestions for next firing:

Kiln Notes
Firing Records

BISQUE

GLAZE

DATE:

OTHER:

FIRING NO.:

CLAY, GLAZES & RECIPES USED

Specific Gravity:

GLAZE TECHNIQUES

SCHEDULE

Ramp 1:

Ramp 2:

Ramp 3:

Ramp 4:

Soak:

Slow cool:

Length of firing hours:

KW used:

Cost:

PACK

Tight

Moderate

Loose

CONES USED

CONE ACHIEVED

GLAZE RESULT

Perfect

Good

OK

Could be better

Disaster

Underfired

Bang on!

Overfired

ADDITIONAL INFO

What went wrong:

What went right:

Suggestions for next firing:

Kiln Notes Firing Records

BISQUE   GLAZE   DATE: ____________

OTHER: ____________   FIRING NO.: ____________

CLAY, GLAZES & RECIPES USED

Specific Gravity:

SCHEDULE

Ramp 1:

Ramp 2:

Ramp 3:

Ramp 4:

Soak:

Slow cool:

Length of firing hours:

KW used:

Cost:

GLAZE TECHNIQUES

PACK

Tight   Moderate   Loose

GLAZE RESULT

Perfect   Underfired

Good   Bang on!

OK   Overfired

Could be better

Disaster

CONES USED

CONE ACHIEVED

ADDITIONAL INFO

What went wrong:

What went right:

Suggestions for next firing:

Kiln Notes Firing Records

BISQUE — GLAZE — DATE: ____________

OTHER: ____________ — FIRING NO.: ____________

CLAY, GLAZES & RECIPES USED

Specific Gravity:

GLAZE TECHNIQUES

SCHEDULE

Ramp 1:

Ramp 2:

Ramp 3:

Ramp 4:

Soak:

Slow cool:

Length of firing hours:

KW used:

Cost:

PACK

Tight — Moderate — Loose

CONES USED

CONE ACHIEVED

GLAZE RESULT

- Perfect
- Good
- OK
- Could be better
- Disaster

- Underfired
- Bang on!
- Overfired

ADDITIONAL INFO

What went wrong:

What went right:

Suggestions for next firing:

Kiln Notes
Firing Records

BISQUE GLAZE DATE: ____________

OTHER: ____________ FIRING NO.: ____________

CLAY, GLAZES & RECIPES USED

Specific Gravity:

SCHEDULE

Ramp 1:

Ramp 2:

Ramp 3:

Ramp 4:

Soak:

Slow cool:

Length of firing hours:

KW used:

Cost:

GLAZE TECHNIQUES

PACK

Tight Moderate Loose

CONES USED

CONE ACHIEVED

GLAZE RESULT

Perfect

Good

OK

Could be better

Disaster

Underfired

Bang on!

Overfired

ADDITIONAL INFO

What went wrong:

What went right:

Suggestions for next firing:

Kiln Notes
Firing Records

BISQUE GLAZE DATE: ______

OTHER: ______ FIRING NO.: ______

CLAY, GLAZES & RECIPES USED

Specific Gravity:

SCHEDULE

Ramp 1:

Ramp 2:

Ramp 3:

Ramp 4:

Soak:

Slow cool:

GLAZE TECHNIQUES

Length of firing hours:

KW used:

Cost:

PACK

Tight Moderate Loose

CONES USED

CONE ACHIEVED

GLAZE RESULT

Perfect

Good

OK

Could be better

Disaster

Underfired

Bang on!

Overfired

ADDITIONAL INFO

What went wrong:

What went right:

Suggestions for next firing:

Kiln Notes Firing Records

BISQUE GLAZE DATE: ______

OTHER: ______ FIRING NO.: ______

CLAY, GLAZES & RECIPES USED

Specific Gravity:

SCHEDULE

Ramp 1:

Ramp 2:

Ramp 3:

Ramp 4:

Soak:

Slow cool:

Length of firing hours:

KW used:

Cost:

GLAZE TECHNIQUES

PACK

Tight Moderate Loose

CONES USED

CONE ACHIEVED

GLAZE RESULT

Perfect Underfired

Good Bang on!

OK Overfired

Could be better

Disaster

ADDITIONAL INFO

What went wrong: What went right: Suggestions for next firing:

Kiln Notes
Firing Records

BISQUE GLAZE DATE: ______

OTHER: ______ FIRING NO.: ______

CLAY, GLAZES & RECIPES USED

Specific Gravity:

SCHEDULE

Ramp 1:

Ramp 2:

Ramp 3:

Ramp 4:

Soak:

Slow cool:

GLAZE TECHNIQUES

Length of firing hours:

KW used:

Cost:

PACK

Tight Moderate Loose

CONES USED

CONE ACHIEVED

GLAZE RESULT

- Perfect
- Good
- OK
- Could be better
- Disaster

- Underfired
- Bang on!
- Overfired

ADDITIONAL INFO

What went wrong:

What went right:

Suggestions for next firing:

Kiln Notes Firing Records

BISQUE GLAZE DATE: ______

OTHER: ______ FIRING NO.: ______

CLAY, GLAZES & RECIPES USED

Specific Gravity:

SCHEDULE

Ramp 1:

Ramp 2:

Ramp 3:

Ramp 4:

Soak:

Slow cool:

Length of firing hours:

KW used:

Cost:

GLAZE TECHNIQUES

PACK

Tight Moderate Loose

GLAZE RESULT

Perfect

Good

OK

Could be better

Disaster

Underfired

Bang on!

Overfired

CONES USED

CONE ACHIEVED

ADDITIONAL INFO

What went wrong:

What went right:

Suggestions for next firing:

Kiln Notes
Firing Records

BISQUE GLAZE DATE: ____________

OTHER: ____________ FIRING NO.: ____________

CLAY, GLAZES & RECIPES USED

Specific Gravity:

SCHEDULE

Ramp 1:

Ramp 2:

Ramp 3:

Ramp 4:

Soak:

Slow cool:

Length of firing hours:

KW used:

Cost:

GLAZE TECHNIQUES

PACK

Tight — Moderate — Loose

CONES USED

CONE ACHIEVED

GLAZE RESULT

- Perfect
- Good
- OK
- Could be better
- Disaster

- Underfired
- Bang on!
- Overfired

ADDITIONAL INFO

What went wrong:

What went right:

Suggestions for next firing:

Kiln Notes
Firing Records

BISQUE GLAZE DATE: ____________

OTHER: ____________ FIRING NO.: ____________

CLAY, GLAZES & RECIPES USED

Specific Gravity:

GLAZE TECHNIQUES

SCHEDULE

Ramp 1:

Ramp 2:

Ramp 3:

Ramp 4:

Soak:

Slow cool:

Length of firing hours:

KW used:

Cost:

PACK

Tight Moderate Loose

CONES USED CONE ACHIEVED

GLAZE RESULT

Perfect

Good

OK

Could be better

Disaster

Underfired

Bang on!

Overfired

ADDITIONAL INFO

What went wrong:

What went right:

Suggestions for next firing:

Kiln Notes Firing Records

BISQUE GLAZE DATE: ____________

OTHER: ____________ FIRING NO.: ____________

CLAY, GLAZES & RECIPES USED

Specific Gravity:

GLAZE TECHNIQUES

SCHEDULE

Ramp 1:

Ramp 2:

Ramp 3:

Ramp 4:

Soak:

Slow cool:

Length of firing hours:

KW used:

Cost:

PACK

Tight Moderate Loose

CONES USED

CONE ACHIEVED

GLAZE RESULT

- Perfect
- Good
- OK
- Could be better
- Disaster

- Underfired
- Bang on!
- Overfired

ADDITIONAL INFO

What went wrong:

What went right:

Suggestions for next firing:

Kiln Notes
Firing Records

BISQUE GLAZE DATE: ________

OTHER: ________ FIRING NO.: ________

CLAY, GLAZES & RECIPES USED

Specific Gravity:

SCHEDULE

Ramp 1:

Ramp 2:

Ramp 3:

Ramp 4:

Soak:

Slow cool:

GLAZE TECHNIQUES

Length of firing hours:

KW used:

Cost:

PACK

Tight Moderate Loose

GLAZE RESULT

Perfect Underfired

Good Bang on!

OK Overfired

Could be better

Disaster

CONES USED CONE ACHIEVED

ADDITIONAL INFO

What went wrong: What went right: Suggestions for next firing:

Kiln Notes
Firing Records

BISQUE   GLAZE   DATE: ____________

OTHER: ____________   FIRING NO.: ____________

CLAY, GLAZES & RECIPES USED

Specific Gravity:

SCHEDULE

Ramp 1:

Ramp 2:

Ramp 3:

Ramp 4:

Soak:

Slow cool:

GLAZE TECHNIQUES

Length of firing hours:

KW used:

Cost:

PACK

Tight   Moderate   Loose

GLAZE RESULT

- Perfect
- Good
- OK
- Could be better
- Disaster

- Underfired
- Bang on!
- Overfired

CONES USED

CONE ACHIEVED

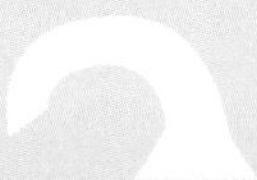

ADDITIONAL INFO

What went wrong:

What went right:

Suggestions for next firing:

Kiln Notes
Firing Records

BISQUE　GLAZE　DATE: ____________

OTHER: ____________　FIRING NO.: ____________

CLAY, GLAZES & RECIPES USED

Specific Gravity:

SCHEDULE

Ramp 1:

Ramp 2:

Ramp 3:

Ramp 4:

Soak:

Slow cool:

GLAZE TECHNIQUES

Length of firing hours:

KW used:

Cost:

PACK

Tight　Moderate　Loose

GLAZE RESULT

- Perfect
- Good
- OK
- Could be better
- Disaster

- Underfired
- Bang on!
- Overfired

CONES USED

CONE ACHIEVED

ADDITIONAL INFO

What went wrong:

What went right:

Suggestions for next firing:

Kiln Notes Firing Records

BISQUE GLAZE DATE: ______________

OTHER: ______________ FIRING NO.: ______________

CLAY, GLAZES & RECIPES USED

Specific Gravity:

SCHEDULE

Ramp 1:

Ramp 2:

Ramp 3:

Ramp 4:

Soak:

Slow cool:

Length of firing hours:

KW used:

Cost:

GLAZE TECHNIQUES

PACK

Tight Moderate Loose

GLAZE RESULT

Perfect

Good

OK

Could be better

Disaster

Underfired

Bang on!

Overfired

CONES USED

CONE ACHIEVED

ADDITIONAL INFO

What went wrong:

What went right:

Suggestions for next firing:

Kiln Notes
Firing Records

BISQUE   GLAZE   DATE: ______

OTHER: ______   FIRING NO.: ______

CLAY, GLAZES & RECIPES USED

Specific Gravity:

SCHEDULE

Ramp 1:

Ramp 2:

Ramp 3:

Ramp 4:

Soak:

Slow cool:

GLAZE TECHNIQUES

Length of firing hours:

KW used:

Cost:

PACK

Tight   Moderate   Loose

GLAZE RESULT

Perfect   Underfired

Good   Bang on!

OK   Overfired

Could be better

Disaster

CONES USED

CONE ACHIEVED

ADDITIONAL INFO

What went wrong:

What went right:

Suggestions for next firing:

Kiln Notes
Firing Records

BISQUE GLAZE DATE: ____________________

OTHER: ________________ FIRING NO.: ____________

CLAY, GLAZES & RECIPES USED

Specific Gravity:

SCHEDULE

Ramp 1:

Ramp 2:

Ramp 3:

Ramp 4:

Soak:

Slow cool:

Length of firing hours:

KW used:

Cost:

GLAZE TECHNIQUES

PACK

Tight — Moderate — Loose

CONES USED

CONE ACHIEVED

GLAZE RESULT

- Perfect
- Good
- OK
- Could be better
- Disaster

- Underfired
- Bang on!
- Overfired

ADDITIONAL INFO

What went wrong:

What went right:

Suggestions for next firing:

Kiln Notes
Firing Records

BISQUE GLAZE DATE: ______

OTHER: ______ FIRING NO.: ______

CLAY, GLAZES & RECIPES USED

Specific Gravity:

GLAZE TECHNIQUES

SCHEDULE

Ramp 1:

Ramp 2:

Ramp 3:

Ramp 4:

Soak:

Slow cool:

Length of firing hours:

KW used:

Cost:

PACK

Tight Moderate Loose

CONES USED

CONE ACHIEVED

GLAZE RESULT

Perfect

Good

OK

Could be better

Disaster

Underfired

Bang on!

Overfired

ADDITIONAL INFO

What went wrong:

What went right:

Suggestions for next firing:

Kiln Notes
Firing Records

BISQUE　GLAZE　DATE: ____________

OTHER: ____________　FIRING NO.: ____________

CLAY, GLAZES & RECIPES USED

Specific Gravity:

SCHEDULE

Ramp 1:

Ramp 2:

Ramp 3:

Ramp 4:

Soak:

Slow cool:

Length of firing hours:

KW used:

Cost:

GLAZE TECHNIQUES

PACK

Tight　Moderate　Loose

GLAZE RESULT

- Perfect
- Good
- OK
- Could be better
- Disaster

- Underfired
- Bang on!
- Overfired

CONES USED

CONE ACHIEVED

ADDITIONAL INFO

What went wrong:

What went right:

Suggestions for next firing:

Kiln Notes
Firing Records

BISQUE GLAZE DATE: ____________

OTHER: ____________ FIRING NO.: ____________

CLAY, GLAZES & RECIPES USED

Specific Gravity:

GLAZE TECHNIQUES

SCHEDULE

Ramp 1:

Ramp 2:

Ramp 3:

Ramp 4:

Soak:

Slow cool:

Length of firing hours:

KW used:

Cost:

PACK

Tight Moderate Loose

CONES USED

CONE ACHIEVED

GLAZE RESULT

Perfect

Good

OK

Could be better

Disaster

Underfired

Bang on!

Overfired

ADDITIONAL INFO

What went wrong:

What went right:

Suggestions for next firing:

Kiln Notes
Firing Records

BISQUE GLAZE DATE: ____________

OTHER: ____________ FIRING NO.: ____________

CLAY, GLAZES & RECIPES USED

Specific Gravity:

GLAZE TECHNIQUES

SCHEDULE

Ramp 1:

Ramp 2:

Ramp 3:

Ramp 4:

Soak:

Slow cool:

Length of firing hours:

KW used:

Cost:

PACK

Tight Moderate Loose

CONES USED

CONE ACHIEVED

GLAZE RESULT

- Perfect
- Good
- OK
- Could be better
- Disaster

- Underfired
- Bang on!
- Overfired

ADDITIONAL INFO

What went wrong:	What went right:	Suggestions for next firing:

Kiln Notes
Firing Records

BISQUE GLAZE DATE: ______

OTHER: ______ FIRING NO.: ______

CLAY, GLAZES & RECIPES USED

Specific Gravity:

SCHEDULE

Ramp 1:

Ramp 2:

Ramp 3:

Ramp 4:

Soak:

Slow cool:

Length of firing hours:

KW used:

Cost:

GLAZE TECHNIQUES

PACK

Tight Moderate Loose

CONES USED

CONE ACHIEVED

GLAZE RESULT

Perfect

Good

OK

Could be better

Disaster

Underfired

Bang on!

Overfired

ADDITIONAL INFO

What went wrong:

What went right:

Suggestions for next firing:

Kiln Notes Firing Records

BISQUE GLAZE DATE: ____________

OTHER: ____________ FIRING NO.: ____________

CLAY, GLAZES & RECIPES USED

Specific Gravity:

SCHEDULE

Ramp 1:

Ramp 2:

Ramp 3:

Ramp 4:

Soak:

Slow cool:

Length of firing hours:

KW used:

Cost:

GLAZE TECHNIQUES

PACK

Tight Moderate Loose

CONES USED

CONE ACHIEVED

GLAZE RESULT

- Perfect
- Good
- OK
- Could be better
- Disaster

- Underfired
- Bang on!
- Overfired

ADDITIONAL INFO

What went wrong:

What went right:

Suggestions for next firing:

Kiln Notes
Firing Records

BISQUE　GLAZE　DATE: ____________

OTHER: ____________　FIRING NO.: ____________

CLAY, GLAZES & RECIPES USED

Specific Gravity:

SCHEDULE

Ramp 1:

Ramp 2:

Ramp 3:

Ramp 4:

Soak:

Slow cool:

Length of firing hours:

KW used:

Cost:

GLAZE TECHNIQUES

PACK

Tight　Moderate　Loose

GLAZE RESULT

Perfect　Underfired

Good　Bang on!

OK　Overfired

Could be better

Disaster

CONES USED

CONE ACHIEVED

ADDITIONAL INFO

What went wrong:

What went right:

Suggestions for next firing:

Kiln Notes
Firing Records

BISQUE GLAZE DATE: ______

OTHER: ______ FIRING NO.: ______

CLAY, GLAZES & RECIPES USED

Specific Gravity:

SCHEDULE

Ramp 1:

Ramp 2:

Ramp 3:

Ramp 4:

Soak:

Slow cool:

Length of firing hours:

KW used:

Cost:

GLAZE TECHNIQUES

PACK

Tight — Moderate — Loose

CONES USED

CONE ACHIEVED

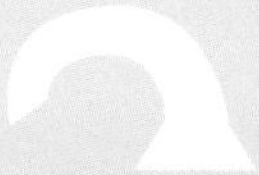

GLAZE RESULT

- Perfect
- Good
- OK
- Could be better
- Disaster

- Underfired
- Bang on!
- Overfired

ADDITIONAL INFO

What went wrong:

What went right:

Suggestions for next firing:

Kiln Notes Firing Records

BISQUE GLAZE DATE: ____________

OTHER: ____________ FIRING NO.: ____________

CLAY, GLAZES & RECIPES USED

Specific Gravity:

GLAZE TECHNIQUES

SCHEDULE

Ramp 1:

Ramp 2:

Ramp 3:

Ramp 4:

Soak:

Slow cool:

Length of firing hours:

KW used:

Cost:

PACK

Tight Moderate Loose

CONES USED

CONE ACHIEVED

GLAZE RESULT

Perfect

Good

OK

Could be better

Disaster

Underfired

Bang on!

Overfired

ADDITIONAL INFO

What went wrong:

What went right:

Suggestions for next firing:

Kiln Notes Firing Records

BISQUE GLAZE DATE: ______

OTHER: ______ FIRING NO.: ______

CLAY, GLAZES & RECIPES USED

Specific Gravity:

GLAZE TECHNIQUES

SCHEDULE

Ramp 1:

Ramp 2:

Ramp 3:

Ramp 4:

Soak:

Slow cool:

Length of firing hours:

KW used:

Cost:

PACK

Tight Moderate Loose

CONES USED

CONE ACHIEVED

GLAZE RESULT

Perfect

Good

OK

Could be better

Disaster

Underfired

Bang on!

Overfired

ADDITIONAL INFO

What went wrong:

What went right:

Suggestions for next firing:

Kiln Notes
Firing Records

BISQUE   GLAZE   DATE: ____________

OTHER: ____________   FIRING NO.: ____________

CLAY, GLAZES & RECIPES USED

Specific Gravity:

GLAZE TECHNIQUES

SCHEDULE

Ramp 1:

Ramp 2:

Ramp 3:

Ramp 4:

Soak:

Slow cool:

Length of firing hours:

KW used:

Cost:

PACK

Tight   Moderate   Loose

CONES USED   CONE ACHIEVED

GLAZE RESULT

Perfect

Good

OK

Could be better

Disaster

Underfired

Bang on!

Overfired

ADDITIONAL INFO

What went wrong:

What went right:

Suggestions for next firing:

Kiln Notes
Firing Records

BISQUE GLAZE DATE: ____________

OTHER: ____________ FIRING NO.: ____________

CLAY, GLAZES & RECIPES USED

Specific Gravity:

SCHEDULE

Ramp 1:

Ramp 2:

Ramp 3:

Ramp 4:

Soak:

Slow cool:

Length of firing hours:

KW used:

Cost:

GLAZE TECHNIQUES

PACK

Tight Moderate Loose

CONES USED

CONE ACHIEVED

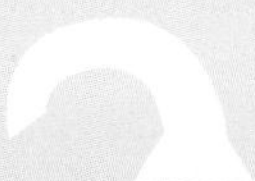

GLAZE RESULT

- Perfect
- Good
- OK
- Could be better
- Disaster

- Underfired
- Bang on!
- Overfired

ADDITIONAL INFO

What went wrong:

What went right:

Suggestions for next firing:

Kiln Notes
Firing Records

BISQUE GLAZE DATE:

OTHER: FIRING NO.:

CLAY, GLAZES & RECIPES USED

Specific Gravity:

SCHEDULE

Ramp 1:

Ramp 2:

Ramp 3:

Ramp 4:

Soak:

Slow cool:

Length of firing hours:

KW used:

Cost:

GLAZE TECHNIQUES

PACK

Tight Moderate Loose

CONES USED CONE ACHIEVED

GLAZE RESULT

Perfect

Good

OK

Could be better

Disaster

Underfired

Bang on!

Overfired

ADDITIONAL INFO

What went wrong:

What went right:

Suggestions for next firing:

Kiln Notes
Firing Records

BISQUE   GLAZE   DATE: ____________

OTHER: ____________   FIRING NO.: ____________

CLAY, GLAZES & RECIPES USED

Specific Gravity:

GLAZE TECHNIQUES

SCHEDULE

Ramp 1:

Ramp 2:

Ramp 3:

Ramp 4:

Soak:

Slow cool:

Length of firing hours:

KW used:

Cost:

PACK

Tight   Moderate   Loose

CONES USED

CONE ACHIEVED

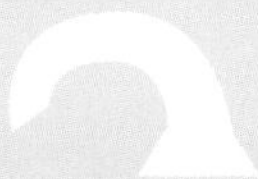

GLAZE RESULT

Perfect

Good

OK

Could be better

Disaster

Underfired

Bang on!

Overfired

ADDITIONAL INFO

What went wrong:

What went right:

Suggestions for next firing:

Kiln Notes Firing Records

BISQUE GLAZE DATE: ____________

OTHER: ____________ FIRING NO.: ____________

CLAY, GLAZES & RECIPES USED

Specific Gravity:

SCHEDULE

Ramp 1:

Ramp 2:

Ramp 3:

Ramp 4:

Soak:

Slow cool:

GLAZE TECHNIQUES

Length of firing hours:

KW used:

Cost:

PACK

Tight Moderate Loose

GLAZE RESULT

Perfect

Good

OK

Could be better

Disaster

Underfired

Bang on!

Overfired

CONES USED

CONE ACHIEVED

ADDITIONAL INFO

What went wrong:

What went right:

Suggestions for next firing:

Kiln Notes
Firing Records

BISQUE GLAZE DATE: ________

OTHER: ________ FIRING NO.: ________

CLAY, GLAZES & RECIPES USED

Specific Gravity:

GLAZE TECHNIQUES

SCHEDULE

Ramp 1:

Ramp 2:

Ramp 3:

Ramp 4:

Soak:

Slow cool:

Length of firing hours:

KW used:

Cost:

PACK

Tight Moderate Loose

CONES USED

CONE ACHIEVED

GLAZE RESULT

Perfect

Good

OK

Could be better

Disaster

Underfired

Bang on!

Overfired

ADDITIONAL INFO

What went wrong:

What went right:

Suggestions for next firing:

Kiln Notes
Firing Records

BISQUE GLAZE DATE:

OTHER: FIRING NO.:

CLAY, GLAZES & RECIPES USED

Specific Gravity:

GLAZE TECHNIQUES

SCHEDULE

Ramp 1:

Ramp 2:

Ramp 3:

Ramp 4:

Soak:

Slow cool:

Length of firing hours:

KW used:

Cost:

PACK

Tight Moderate Loose

CONES USED

CONE ACHIEVED

GLAZE RESULT

Perfect

Good

OK

Could be better

Disaster

Underfired

Bang on!

Overfired

ADDITIONAL INFO

What went wrong:

What went right:

Suggestions for next firing:

Kiln Notes
Firing Records

BISQUE

GLAZE

DATE: ______________

OTHER: ______________

FIRING NO.: ______________

CLAY, GLAZES & RECIPES USED

Specific Gravity:

SCHEDULE

Ramp 1:

Ramp 2:

Ramp 3:

Ramp 4:

Soak:

Slow cool:

GLAZE TECHNIQUES

Length of firing hours:

KW used:

Cost:

PACK

Tight — Moderate — Loose

GLAZE RESULT

- Perfect
- Good
- OK
- Could be better
- Disaster

- Underfired
- Bang on!
- Overfired

CONES USED

CONE ACHIEVED

ADDITIONAL INFO

What went wrong:

What went right:

Suggestions for next firing:

Kiln Notes Firing Records

BISQUE   GLAZE   DATE: ____________

OTHER: ____________   FIRING NO.: ____________

CLAY, GLAZES & RECIPES USED

Specific Gravity:

SCHEDULE

Ramp 1:

Ramp 2:

Ramp 3:

Ramp 4:

Soak:

Slow cool:

Length of firing hours:

KW used:

Cost:

GLAZE TECHNIQUES

PACK

Tight   Moderate   Loose

GLAZE RESULT

Perfect

Good

OK

Could be better

Disaster

Underfired

Bang on!

Overfired

CONES USED

CONE ACHIEVED

ADDITIONAL INFO

What went wrong:

What went right:

Suggestions for next firing:

Kiln Notes
Firing Records

BISQUE GLAZE DATE: ______________

OTHER: ______________ FIRING NO.: ______________

CLAY, GLAZES & RECIPES USED

Specific Gravity:

GLAZE TECHNIQUES

SCHEDULE

Ramp 1:

Ramp 2:

Ramp 3:

Ramp 4:

Soak:

Slow cool:

Length of firing hours:

KW used:

Cost:

PACK

Tight Moderate Loose

CONES USED

CONE ACHIEVED

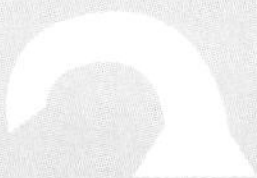

GLAZE RESULT

Perfect

Good

OK

Could be better

Disaster

Underfired

Bang on!

Overfired

ADDITIONAL INFO

What went wrong:

What went right:

Suggestions for next firing:

Kiln Notes
Firing Records

BISQUE

GLAZE

DATE: ____________

OTHER: ____________

FIRING NO.: ____________

CLAY, GLAZES & RECIPES USED

Specific Gravity:

SCHEDULE

Ramp 1:

Ramp 2:

Ramp 3:

Ramp 4:

Soak:

Slow cool:

GLAZE TECHNIQUES

Length of firing hours:

KW used:

Cost:

PACK

Tight

Moderate

Loose

GLAZE RESULT

Perfect

Good

OK

Could be better

Disaster

Underfired

Bang on!

Overfired

CONES USED

CONE ACHIEVED

ADDITIONAL INFO

What went wrong:

What went right:

Suggestions for next firing:

Kiln Notes Firing Records

BISQUE GLAZE DATE: ____________

OTHER: ____________ FIRING NO.: ____________

CLAY, GLAZES & RECIPES USED

Specific Gravity:

SCHEDULE

Ramp 1:

Ramp 2:

Ramp 3:

Ramp 4:

Soak:

Slow cool:

GLAZE TECHNIQUES

Length of firing hours:

KW used:

Cost:

PACK

Tight — Moderate — Loose

GLAZE RESULT

- Perfect
- Good
- OK
- Could be better
- Disaster

- Underfired
- Bang on!
- Overfired

CONES USED

CONE ACHIEVED

ADDITIONAL INFO

What went wrong:

What went right:

Suggestions for next firing:

Kiln Notes
Firing Records

BISQUE GLAZE DATE: ______

OTHER: ______ FIRING NO.: ______

CLAY, GLAZES & RECIPES USED

Specific Gravity:

SCHEDULE

Ramp 1:

Ramp 2:

Ramp 3:

Ramp 4:

Soak:

Slow cool:

GLAZE TECHNIQUES

Length of firing hours:

KW used:

Cost:

PACK

Tight Moderate Loose

CONES USED CONE ACHIEVED

GLAZE RESULT

Perfect

Good

OK

Could be better

Disaster

Underfired

Bang on!

Overfired

ADDITIONAL INFO

What went wrong:

What went right:

Suggestions for next firing:

Kiln Notes
Firing Records

BISQUE GLAZE DATE: ____________

OTHER: ____________ FIRING NO.: ____________

CLAY, GLAZES & RECIPES USED

Specific Gravity:

GLAZE TECHNIQUES

SCHEDULE

Ramp 1:

Ramp 2:

Ramp 3:

Ramp 4:

Soak:

Slow cool:

Length of firing hours:

KW used:

Cost:

PACK

Tight Moderate Loose

CONES USED

CONE ACHIEVED

GLAZE RESULT

Perfect

Good

OK

Could be better

Disaster

Underfired

Bang on!

Overfired

ADDITIONAL INFO

What went wrong:

What went right:

Suggestions for next firing:

Kiln Notes
Firing Records

BISQUE GLAZE DATE: ____________

OTHER: ____________ FIRING NO.: ____________

CLAY, GLAZES & RECIPES USED

Specific Gravity:

SCHEDULE

Ramp 1:

Ramp 2:

Ramp 3:

Ramp 4:

Soak:

Slow cool:

GLAZE TECHNIQUES

Length of firing hours:

KW used:

Cost:

PACK

Tight Moderate Loose

GLAZE RESULT

Perfect

Good

OK

Could be better

Disaster

Underfired

Bang on!

Overfired

CONES USED

CONE ACHIEVED

ADDITIONAL INFO

What went wrong:

What went right:

Suggestions for next firing:

Kiln Notes Firing Records

BISQUE GLAZE DATE: ____________

OTHER: ____________ FIRING NO.: ____________

CLAY, GLAZES & RECIPES USED

Specific Gravity:

GLAZE TECHNIQUES

SCHEDULE

Ramp 1:

Ramp 2:

Ramp 3:

Ramp 4:

Soak:

Slow cool:

Length of firing hours:

KW used:

Cost:

PACK

Tight Moderate Loose

CONES USED

CONE ACHIEVED

GLAZE RESULT

- Perfect
- Good
- OK
- Could be better
- Disaster

- Underfired
- Bang on!
- Overfired

ADDITIONAL INFO

What went wrong:

What went right:

Suggestions for next firing:

Kiln Notes
Firing Records

BISQUE GLAZE DATE: ______

OTHER: ______ FIRING NO.: ______

CLAY, GLAZES & RECIPES USED

Specific Gravity:

GLAZE TECHNIQUES

SCHEDULE

Ramp 1:

Ramp 2:

Ramp 3:

Ramp 4:

Soak:

Slow cool:

Length of firing hours:

KW used:

Cost:

PACK

Tight Moderate Loose

CONES USED CONE ACHIEVED

GLAZE RESULT

Perfect

Good

OK

Could be better

Disaster

Underfired

Bang on!

Overfired

ADDITIONAL INFO

What went wrong:

What went right:

Suggestions for next firing:

Kiln Notes
Firing Records

BISQUE GLAZE DATE: ________________

OTHER: ____________ FIRING NO.: __________

CLAY, GLAZES & RECIPES USED

Specific Gravity:

GLAZE TECHNIQUES

SCHEDULE

Ramp 1:

Ramp 2:

Ramp 3:

Ramp 4:

Soak:

Slow cool:

Length of firing hours:

KW used:

Cost:

PACK

Tight Moderate Loose

CONES USED

CONE ACHIEVED

GLAZE RESULT

Perfect

Good

OK

Could be better

Disaster

Underfired

Bang on!

Overfired

ADDITIONAL INFO

What went wrong:

What went right:

Suggestions for next firing:

Kiln Notes
Firing Records

BISQUE   GLAZE   DATE: ______

OTHER: ______   FIRING NO.: ______

CLAY, GLAZES & RECIPES USED

Specific Gravity:

GLAZE TECHNIQUES

SCHEDULE

Ramp 1:

Ramp 2:

Ramp 3:

Ramp 4:

Soak:

Slow cool:

Length of firing hours:

KW used:

Cost:

PACK

Tight   Moderate   Loose

CONES USED

CONE ACHIEVED

GLAZE RESULT

Perfect

Good

OK

Could be better

Disaster

Underfired

Bang on!

Overfired

ADDITIONAL INFO

What went wrong:

What went right:

Suggestions for next firing:

Kiln Notes
Firing Records

BISQUE   GLAZE   DATE: ____________

OTHER: ____________   FIRING NO.: ____________

CLAY, GLAZES & RECIPES USED

Specific Gravity:

SCHEDULE

Ramp 1:

Ramp 2:

Ramp 3:

Ramp 4:

Soak:

Slow cool:

GLAZE TECHNIQUES

Length of firing hours:

KW used:

Cost:

PACK

Tight   Moderate   Loose

GLAZE RESULT

Perfect

Good

OK

Could be better

Disaster

Underfired

Bang on!

Overfired

CONES USED

CONE ACHIEVED

ADDITIONAL INFO

What went wrong:

What went right:

Suggestions for next firing:

Kiln Notes Firing Records

BISQUE GLAZE DATE: ____________

OTHER: ____________ FIRING NO.: ____________

CLAY, GLAZES & RECIPES USED

Specific Gravity:

SCHEDULE

Ramp 1:

Ramp 2:

Ramp 3:

Ramp 4:

Soak:

Slow cool:

GLAZE TECHNIQUES

Length of firing hours:

KW used:

Cost:

PACK

Tight Moderate Loose

GLAZE RESULT

Perfect

Good

OK

Could be better

Disaster

Underfired

Bang on!

Overfired

CONES USED

CONE ACHIEVED

ADDITIONAL INFO

What went wrong:

What went right:

Suggestions for next firing:

Kiln Notes
Firing Records

BISQUE

GLAZE

DATE: ____________________

OTHER: ________________

FIRING NO.: ____________

CLAY, GLAZES & RECIPES USED

Specific Gravity:

GLAZE TECHNIQUES

SCHEDULE

Ramp 1:

Ramp 2:

Ramp 3:

Ramp 4:

Soak:

Slow cool:

Length of firing hours:

KW used:

Cost:

PACK

Tight — Moderate — Loose

CONES USED

CONE ACHIEVED

GLAZE RESULT

- Perfect
- Good
- OK
- Could be better
- Disaster

- Underfired
- Bang on!
- Overfired

ADDITIONAL INFO

What went wrong:

What went right:

Suggestions for next firing:

Kiln Notes
Firing Records

BISQUE   GLAZE   DATE: ____________

OTHER: ____________   FIRING NO.: ____________

CLAY, GLAZES & RECIPES USED

Specific Gravity:

SCHEDULE

Ramp 1:

Ramp 2:

Ramp 3:

Ramp 4:

Soak:

Slow cool:

GLAZE TECHNIQUES

Length of firing hours:

KW used:

Cost:

PACK

Tight   Moderate   Loose

GLAZE RESULT

Perfect

Good

OK

Could be better

Disaster

Underfired

Bang on!

Overfired

CONES USED

CONE ACHIEVED

ADDITIONAL INFO

What went wrong:

What went right:

Suggestions for next firing:

Kiln Notes
Firing Records

BISQUE GLAZE DATE: ____________

OTHER: ____________ FIRING NO.: ____________

CLAY, GLAZES & RECIPES USED

Specific Gravity:

GLAZE TECHNIQUES

SCHEDULE

Ramp 1:

Ramp 2:

Ramp 3:

Ramp 4:

Soak:

Slow cool:

Length of firing hours:

KW used:

Cost:

PACK

Tight — Moderate — Loose

CONES USED

CONE ACHIEVED

GLAZE RESULT

- Perfect
- Good
- OK
- Could be better
- Disaster

- Underfired
- Bang on!
- Overfired

ADDITIONAL INFO

What went wrong:

What went right:

Suggestions for next firing:

Kiln Notes Firing Records

BISQUE GLAZE DATE: ______

OTHER: ______ FIRING NO.: ______

CLAY, GLAZES & RECIPES USED

Specific Gravity:

SCHEDULE

Ramp 1:

Ramp 2:

Ramp 3:

Ramp 4:

Soak:

Slow cool:

Length of firing hours:

KW used:

Cost:

GLAZE TECHNIQUES

PACK

Tight Moderate Loose

CONES USED

CONE ACHIEVED

GLAZE RESULT

Perfect

Good

OK

Could be better

Disaster

Underfired

Bang on!

Overfired

ADDITIONAL INFO

What went wrong:

What went right:

Suggestions for next firing:

Kiln Notes Firing Records

BISQUE GLAZE DATE: ______________

OTHER: ______________ FIRING NO.: ______________

CLAY, GLAZES & RECIPES USED

Specific Gravity:

SCHEDULE

Ramp 1:

Ramp 2:

Ramp 3:

Ramp 4:

Soak:

Slow cool:

GLAZE TECHNIQUES

Length of firing hours:

KW used:

Cost:

PACK

Tight Moderate Loose

GLAZE RESULT

Perfect

Good

OK

Could be better

Disaster

Underfired

Bang on!

Overfired

CONES USED

CONE ACHIEVED

ADDITIONAL INFO

What went wrong:

What went right:

Suggestions for next firing:

Kiln Notes
Firing Records

BISQUE   GLAZE   DATE: ____________

OTHER: ____________   FIRING NO.: ____________

CLAY, GLAZES & RECIPES USED

Specific Gravity:

SCHEDULE

Ramp 1:

Ramp 2:

Ramp 3:

Ramp 4:

Soak:

Slow cool:

Length of firing hours:

KW used:

Cost:

GLAZE TECHNIQUES

PACK

Tight   Moderate   Loose

GLAZE RESULT

Perfect

Good

OK

Could be better

Disaster

Underfired

Bang on!

Overfired

CONES USED

CONE ACHIEVED

ADDITIONAL INFO

What went wrong:

What went right:

Suggestions for next firing:

Kiln Notes
Firing Records

○ BISQUE ○ GLAZE DATE: ______________

○ OTHER: ______________ FIRING NO.: ______________

CLAY, GLAZES & RECIPES USED

Specific Gravity:

GLAZE TECHNIQUES

SCHEDULE

Ramp 1:

Ramp 2:

Ramp 3:

Ramp 4:

Soak:

Slow cool:

Length of firing hours:

KW used:

Cost:

PACK

Tight — Moderate — Loose

CONES USED

CONE ACHIEVED

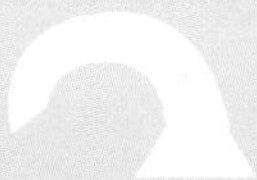

GLAZE RESULT

- Perfect
- Good
- OK
- Could be better
- Disaster

- Underfired
- Bang on!
- Overfired

ADDITIONAL INFO

What went wrong:

What went right:

Suggestions for next firing:

Kiln Notes
Firing Records

BISQUE GLAZE DATE: ______

OTHER: ______ FIRING NO.: ______

CLAY, GLAZES & RECIPES USED

Specific Gravity:

GLAZE TECHNIQUES

SCHEDULE

Ramp 1:

Ramp 2:

Ramp 3:

Ramp 4:

Soak:

Slow cool:

Length of firing hours:

KW used:

Cost:

PACK

Tight Moderate Loose

CONES USED

CONE ACHIEVED

GLAZE RESULT

Perfect

Good

OK

Could be better

Disaster

Underfired

Bang on!

Overfired

ADDITIONAL INFO

What went wrong:

What went right:

Suggestions for next firing:

Kiln Notes
Firing Records

BISQUE   GLAZE   DATE: ______

OTHER: ______   FIRING NO.: ______

CLAY, GLAZES & RECIPES USED

Specific Gravity:

SCHEDULE

Ramp 1:

Ramp 2:

Ramp 3:

Ramp 4:

Soak:

Slow cool:

Length of firing hours:

KW used:

Cost:

GLAZE TECHNIQUES

PACK

Tight — Moderate — Loose

GLAZE RESULT

- Perfect
- Good
- OK
- Could be better
- Disaster

- Underfired
- Bang on!
- Overfired

CONES USED

CONE ACHIEVED

ADDITIONAL INFO

What went wrong:

What went right:

Suggestions for next firing:

Kiln Notes Firing Records

BISQUE GLAZE DATE: ____________

OTHER: ____________ FIRING NO.: ____________

CLAY, GLAZES & RECIPES USED

Specific Gravity:

SCHEDULE

Ramp 1:

Ramp 2:

Ramp 3:

Ramp 4:

Soak:

Slow cool:

Length of firing hours:

KW used:

Cost:

GLAZE TECHNIQUES

PACK

Tight Moderate Loose

GLAZE RESULT

Perfect Underfired

Good Bang on!

OK Overfired

Could be better

Disaster

CONES USED

CONE ACHIEVED

ADDITIONAL INFO

What went wrong:

What went right:

Suggestions for next firing:

Kiln Notes
Firing Records

BISQUE GLAZE DATE: ____________

OTHER: ____________ FIRING NO.: ____________

CLAY, GLAZES & RECIPES USED

Specific Gravity:

GLAZE TECHNIQUES

SCHEDULE

Ramp 1:

Ramp 2:

Ramp 3:

Ramp 4:

Soak:

Slow cool:

Length of firing hours:

KW used:

Cost:

PACK

Tight Moderate Loose

CONES USED

CONE ACHIEVED

GLAZE RESULT

Perfect

Good

OK

Could be better

Disaster

Underfired

Bang on!

Overfired

ADDITIONAL INFO

What went wrong:

What went right:

Suggestions for next firing:

Kiln Notes
Firing Records

BISQUE GLAZE DATE: ______

OTHER: ______ FIRING NO.: ______

CLAY, GLAZES & RECIPES USED

Specific Gravity:

GLAZE TECHNIQUES

SCHEDULE

Ramp 1:

Ramp 2:

Ramp 3:

Ramp 4:

Soak:

Slow cool:

Length of firing hours:

KW used:

Cost:

PACK

Tight Moderate Loose

CONES USED

CONE ACHIEVED

GLAZE RESULT

Perfect

Good

OK

Could be better

Disaster

Underfired

Bang on!

Overfired

ADDITIONAL INFO

What went wrong:

What went right:

Suggestions for next firing:

Kiln Notes Firing Records

BISQUE GLAZE DATE: ______________

OTHER: ______________ FIRING NO.: ______________

CLAY, GLAZES & RECIPES USED

Specific Gravity:

GLAZE TECHNIQUES

SCHEDULE

Ramp 1:

Ramp 2:

Ramp 3:

Ramp 4:

Soak:

Slow cool:

Length of firing hours:

KW used:

Cost:

PACK

Tight — Moderate — Loose

CONES USED

CONE ACHIEVED

GLAZE RESULT

- Perfect
- Good
- OK
- Could be better
- Disaster

- Underfired
- Bang on!
- Overfired

ADDITIONAL INFO

What went wrong:

What went right:

Suggestions for next firing:

Kiln Notes
Firing Records

BISQUE GLAZE DATE: ______________

OTHER: ______________ FIRING NO.: ______________

CLAY, GLAZES & RECIPES USED

Specific Gravity:

GLAZE TECHNIQUES

SCHEDULE

Ramp 1:

Ramp 2:

Ramp 3:

Ramp 4:

Soak:

Slow cool:

Length of firing hours:

KW used:

Cost:

PACK

Tight Moderate Loose

CONES USED

CONE ACHIEVED

GLAZE RESULT

Perfect

Good

OK

Could be better

Disaster

Underfired

Bang on!

Overfired

ADDITIONAL INFO

What went wrong:

What went right:

Suggestions for next firing:

Kiln Notes
Firing Records

BISQUE GLAZE DATE: ________

OTHER: ________ FIRING NO.: ________

CLAY, GLAZES & RECIPES USED

Specific Gravity:

SCHEDULE

Ramp 1:

Ramp 2:

Ramp 3:

Ramp 4:

Soak:

Slow cool:

GLAZE TECHNIQUES

Length of firing hours:

KW used:

Cost:

PACK

Tight Moderate Loose

CONES USED

CONE ACHIEVED

GLAZE RESULT

Perfect

Good

OK

Could be better

Disaster

Underfired

Bang on!

Overfired

ADDITIONAL INFO

What went wrong:

What went right:

Suggestions for next firing:

Kiln Notes
Firing Records

BISQUE GLAZE DATE: ____________

OTHER: ____________ FIRING NO.: ____________

CLAY, GLAZES & RECIPES USED

Specific Gravity:

SCHEDULE

Ramp 1:

Ramp 2:

Ramp 3:

Ramp 4:

Soak:

Slow cool:

GLAZE TECHNIQUES

Length of firing hours:

KW used:

Cost:

PACK

Tight Moderate Loose

GLAZE RESULT

Perfect

Good

OK

Could be better

Disaster

Underfired

Bang on!

Overfired

CONES USED

CONE ACHIEVED

ADDITIONAL INFO

What went wrong:

What went right:

Suggestions for next firing:

Kiln Notes
Firing Records

BISQUE   GLAZE   DATE: ______________

OTHER: ______________   FIRING NO.: ______________

CLAY, GLAZES & RECIPES USED

Specific Gravity:

SCHEDULE

Ramp 1:

Ramp 2:

Ramp 3:

Ramp 4:

Soak:

Slow cool:

GLAZE TECHNIQUES

Length of firing hours:

KW used:

Cost:

PACK

Tight   Moderate   Loose

GLAZE RESULT

Perfect

Good

OK

Could be better

Disaster

Underfired

Bang on!

Overfired

CONES USED

CONE ACHIEVED

ADDITIONAL INFO

What went wrong:

What went right:

Suggestions for next firing:

Kiln Notes
Firing Records

BISQUE GLAZE DATE: ______

OTHER: ______ FIRING NO.: ______

CLAY, GLAZES & RECIPES USED

Specific Gravity:

GLAZE TECHNIQUES

SCHEDULE

Ramp 1:

Ramp 2:

Ramp 3:

Ramp 4:

Soak:

Slow cool:

Length of firing hours:

KW used:

Cost:

PACK

Tight Moderate Loose

CONES USED

CONE ACHIEVED

GLAZE RESULT

Perfect

Good

OK

Could be better

Disaster

Underfired

Bang on!

Overfired

ADDITIONAL INFO

What went wrong:

What went right:

Suggestions for next firing:

Kiln Notes Firing Records

BISQUE   GLAZE   DATE: ____________

OTHER: ____________   FIRING NO.: ____________

CLAY, GLAZES & RECIPES USED

Specific Gravity:

SCHEDULE

Ramp 1:

Ramp 2:

Ramp 3:

Ramp 4:

Soak:

Slow cool:

Length of firing hours:

KW used:

Cost:

GLAZE TECHNIQUES

PACK

Tight   Moderate   Loose

CONES USED

CONE ACHIEVED

GLAZE RESULT

Perfect

Good

OK

Could be better

Disaster

Underfired

Bang on!

Overfired

ADDITIONAL INFO

What went wrong:

What went right:

Suggestions for next firing:

Kiln Notes Firing Records

BISQUE GLAZE DATE: ____________

OTHER: ____________ FIRING NO.: ____________

CLAY, GLAZES & RECIPES USED

Specific Gravity:

GLAZE TECHNIQUES

SCHEDULE

Ramp 1:

Ramp 2:

Ramp 3:

Ramp 4:

Soak:

Slow cool:

Length of firing hours:

KW used:

Cost:

PACK

Tight Moderate Loose

CONES USED

CONE ACHIEVED

GLAZE RESULT

Perfect

Good

OK

Could be better

Disaster

Underfired

Bang on!

Overfired

ADDITIONAL INFO

What went wrong:

What went right:

Suggestions for next firing:

Kiln Notes
Firing Records

BISQUE GLAZE DATE: ____________

OTHER: ____________ FIRING NO.: ____________

CLAY, GLAZES & RECIPES USED

Specific Gravity:

SCHEDULE

Ramp 1:

Ramp 2:

Ramp 3:

Ramp 4:

Soak:

Slow cool:

Length of firing hours:

KW used:

Cost:

GLAZE TECHNIQUES

PACK

Tight Moderate Loose

GLAZE RESULT

Perfect

Good

OK

Could be better

Disaster

Underfired

Bang on!

Overfired

CONES USED

CONE ACHIEVED

ADDITIONAL INFO

What went wrong:

What went right:

Suggestions for next firing:

Kiln Notes
Firing Records

BISQUE   GLAZE   DATE: ____________

OTHER: ____________   FIRING NO.: ____________

CLAY, GLAZES & RECIPES USED

Specific Gravity:

SCHEDULE

Ramp 1:

Ramp 2:

Ramp 3:

Ramp 4:

Soak:

Slow cool:

Length of firing hours:

KW used:

Cost:

GLAZE TECHNIQUES

PACK

Tight   Moderate   Loose

CONES USED   CONE ACHIEVED

GLAZE RESULT

Perfect

Good

OK

Could be better

Disaster

Underfired

Bang on!

Overfired

ADDITIONAL INFO

What went wrong: What went right: Suggestions for next firing:

Kiln Notes
Firing Records

BISQUE GLAZE DATE: ____________

OTHER: ____________ FIRING NO.: ____________

CLAY, GLAZES & RECIPES USED

Specific Gravity:

GLAZE TECHNIQUES

SCHEDULE

Ramp 1:

Ramp 2:

Ramp 3:

Ramp 4:

Soak:

Slow cool:

Length of firing hours:

KW used:

Cost:

PACK

Tight Moderate Loose

CONES USED

CONE ACHIEVED

GLAZE RESULT

Perfect

Good

OK

Could be better

Disaster

Underfired

Bang on!

Overfired

ADDITIONAL INFO

What went wrong:

What went right:

Suggestions for next firing:

Kiln Notes
Firing Records

BISQUE | GLAZE | DATE: ____________

OTHER: ____________ | FIRING NO.: ____________

CLAY, GLAZES & RECIPES USED

Specific Gravity:

SCHEDULE

Ramp 1:

Ramp 2:

Ramp 3:

Ramp 4:

Soak:

Slow cool:

GLAZE TECHNIQUES

Length of firing hours:

KW used:

Cost:

PACK

Tight | Moderate | Loose

CONES USED

CONE ACHIEVED

GLAZE RESULT

Perfect

Good

OK

Could be better

Disaster

Underfired

Bang on!

Overfired

ADDITIONAL INFO

What went wrong:

What went right:

Suggestions for next firing:

Kiln Notes
Firing Records

BISQUE | GLAZE | DATE: ____________

OTHER: ____________ | FIRING NO.: ____________

CLAY, GLAZES & RECIPES USED

Specific Gravity:

SCHEDULE

Ramp 1:

Ramp 2:

Ramp 3:

Ramp 4:

Soak:

Slow cool:

GLAZE TECHNIQUES

Length of firing hours:

KW used:

Cost:

PACK

Tight | Moderate | Loose

GLAZE RESULT

Perfect

Good

OK

Could be better

Disaster

Underfired

Bang on!

Overfired

CONES USED

CONE ACHIEVED

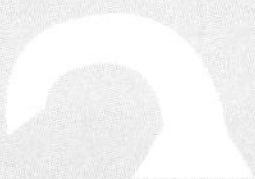

ADDITIONAL INFO

What went wrong:

What went right:

Suggestions for next firing:

Kiln Notes Firing Records

BISQUE   GLAZE   DATE: ______

OTHER: ______   FIRING NO.: ______

CLAY, GLAZES & RECIPES USED

Specific Gravity:

SCHEDULE

Ramp 1:

Ramp 2:

Ramp 3:

Ramp 4:

Soak:

Slow cool:

Length of firing hours:

KW used:

Cost:

GLAZE TECHNIQUES

PACK

Tight   Moderate   Loose

GLAZE RESULT

Perfect   Underfired

Good   Bang on!

OK   Overfired

Could be better

Disaster

CONES USED   CONE ACHIEVED

ADDITIONAL INFO

What went wrong: What went right: Suggestions for next firing:

Kiln Notes
Firing Records

BISQUE   GLAZE   DATE: ____________

OTHER: ____________   FIRING NO.: ____________

CLAY, GLAZES & RECIPES USED

Specific Gravity:

SCHEDULE

Ramp 1:

Ramp 2:

Ramp 3:

Ramp 4:

Soak:

Slow cool:

Length of firing hours:

KW used:

Cost:

GLAZE TECHNIQUES

PACK

Tight   Moderate   Loose

GLAZE RESULT

Perfect

Good

OK

Could be better

Disaster

Underfired

Bang on!

Overfired

CONES USED

CONE ACHIEVED

ADDITIONAL INFO

What went wrong:

What went right:

Suggestions for next firing:

Kiln Notes
Firing Records

BISQUE GLAZE DATE: ______

OTHER: ______ FIRING NO.: ______

CLAY, GLAZES & RECIPES USED

Specific Gravity:

GLAZE TECHNIQUES

SCHEDULE

Ramp 1:

Ramp 2:

Ramp 3:

Ramp 4:

Soak:

Slow cool:

Length of firing hours:

KW used:

Cost:

PACK

Tight Moderate Loose

CONES USED CONE ACHIEVED

GLAZE RESULT

Perfect

Good

OK

Could be better

Disaster

Underfired

Bang on!

Overfired

ADDITIONAL INFO

What went wrong:

What went right:

Suggestions for next firing:

Kiln Notes
Firing Records

BISQUE   GLAZE   DATE: ____________

OTHER: ____________   FIRING NO.: ____________

CLAY, GLAZES & RECIPES USED

Specific Gravity:

GLAZE TECHNIQUES

SCHEDULE

Ramp 1:

Ramp 2:

Ramp 3:

Ramp 4:

Soak:

Slow cool:

Length of firing hours:

KW used:

Cost:

PACK

Tight   Moderate   Loose

CONES USED

CONE ACHIEVED

GLAZE RESULT

Perfect

Good

OK

Could be better

Disaster

Underfired

Bang on!

Overfired

ADDITIONAL INFO

What went wrong:

What went right:

Suggestions for next firing:

Kiln Notes Firing Records

BISQUE GLAZE DATE: ____________

OTHER: ____________ FIRING NO.: ____________

CLAY, GLAZES & RECIPES USED

Specific Gravity:

SCHEDULE

Ramp 1:

Ramp 2:

Ramp 3:

Ramp 4:

Soak:

Slow cool:

Length of firing hours:

KW used:

Cost:

GLAZE TECHNIQUES

PACK

Tight Moderate Loose

CONES USED

CONE ACHIEVED

GLAZE RESULT

Perfect

Good

OK

Could be better

Disaster

Underfired

Bang on!

Overfired

ADDITIONAL INFO

What went wrong:

What went right:

Suggestions for next firing:

Kiln Notes
Firing Records

BISQUE GLAZE DATE:

OTHER: FIRING NO.:

CLAY, GLAZES & RECIPES USED

Specific Gravity:

SCHEDULE

Ramp 1:

Ramp 2:

Ramp 3:

Ramp 4:

Soak:

Slow cool:

GLAZE TECHNIQUES

Length of firing hours:

KW used:

Cost:

PACK

Tight Moderate Loose

CONES USED

CONE ACHIEVED

GLAZE RESULT

Perfect

Good

OK

Could be better

Disaster

Underfired

Bang on!

Overfired

ADDITIONAL INFO

What went wrong:

What went right:

Suggestions for next firing:

Kiln Notes Firing Records

BISQUE GLAZE DATE: ______

OTHER: ______ FIRING NO.: ______

CLAY, GLAZES & RECIPES USED

Specific Gravity:

GLAZE TECHNIQUES

SCHEDULE

Ramp 1:

Ramp 2:

Ramp 3:

Ramp 4:

Soak:

Slow cool:

Length of firing hours:

KW used:

Cost:

PACK

Tight Moderate Loose

CONES USED CONE ACHIEVED

GLAZE RESULT

Perfect

Underfired

Good

Bang on!

OK

Overfired

Could be better

Disaster

ADDITIONAL INFO

What went wrong:

What went right:

Suggestions for next firing:

Kiln Notes
Firing Records

BISQUE ○ GLAZE ○ DATE: ______________

OTHER: ______________ FIRING NO.: ______________

CLAY, GLAZES & RECIPES USED

Specific Gravity:

SCHEDULE

Ramp 1:

Ramp 2:

Ramp 3:

Ramp 4:

Soak:

Slow cool:

Length of firing hours:

KW used:

Cost:

GLAZE TECHNIQUES

PACK

Tight — Moderate — Loose

GLAZE RESULT

- Perfect
- Good
- OK
- Could be better
- Disaster

- Underfired
- Bang on!
- Overfired

CONES USED

CONE ACHIEVED

ADDITIONAL INFO

What went wrong:

What went right:

Suggestions for next firing:

Kiln Notes Firing Records

BISQUE GLAZE DATE: ____________

OTHER: ____________ FIRING NO.: ____________

CLAY, GLAZES & RECIPES USED

Specific Gravity:

SCHEDULE

Ramp 1:

Ramp 2:

Ramp 3:

Ramp 4:

Soak:

Slow cool:

GLAZE TECHNIQUES

Length of firing hours:

KW used:

Cost:

PACK

Tight Moderate Loose

GLAZE RESULT

Perfect

Good

OK

Could be better

Disaster

Underfired

Bang on!

Overfired

CONES USED

CONE ACHIEVED

ADDITIONAL INFO

What went wrong:

What went right:

Suggestions for next firing:

Kiln Notes
Firing Records

BISQUE GLAZE DATE: ____________

OTHER: ____________ FIRING NO.: ____________

CLAY, GLAZES & RECIPES USED

Specific Gravity:

GLAZE TECHNIQUES

SCHEDULE

Ramp 1:

Ramp 2:

Ramp 3:

Ramp 4:

Soak:

Slow cool:

Length of firing hours:

KW used:

Cost:

PACK

Tight — Moderate — Loose

CONES USED

CONE ACHIEVED

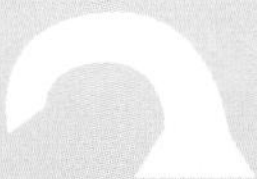

GLAZE RESULT

- Perfect
- Good
- OK
- Could be better
- Disaster

- Underfired
- Bang on!
- Overfired

ADDITIONAL INFO

What went wrong:

What went right:

Suggestions for next firing:

Kiln Notes
Firing Records

BISQUE   GLAZE   DATE: ______

OTHER: ______   FIRING NO.: ______

CLAY, GLAZES & RECIPES USED

Specific Gravity:

GLAZE TECHNIQUES

SCHEDULE

Ramp 1:

Ramp 2:

Ramp 3:

Ramp 4:

Soak:

Slow cool:

Length of firing hours:

KW used:

Cost:

PACK

Tight — Moderate — Loose

CONES USED

CONE ACHIEVED

GLAZE RESULT

Perfect

Good

OK

Could be better

Disaster

Underfired

Bang on!

Overfired

ADDITIONAL INFO

What went wrong:

What went right:

Suggestions for next firing:

Kiln Notes Firing Records

BISQUE GLAZE DATE: ____________

OTHER: ____________ FIRING NO.: ____________

CLAY, GLAZES & RECIPES USED

Specific Gravity:

GLAZE TECHNIQUES

SCHEDULE

Ramp 1:

Ramp 2:

Ramp 3:

Ramp 4:

Soak:

Slow cool:

Length of firing hours:

KW used:

Cost:

PACK

Tight Moderate Loose

CONES USED

CONE ACHIEVED

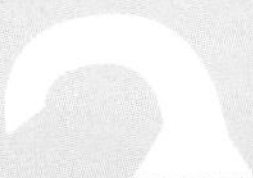

GLAZE RESULT

- Perfect
- Good
- OK
- Could be better
- Disaster

- Underfired
- Bang on!
- Overfired

ADDITIONAL INFO

What went wrong:

What went right:

Suggestions for next firing:

Kiln Notes
Firing Records

BISQUE GLAZE DATE: ____________

OTHER: ____________ FIRING NO.: ____________

CLAY, GLAZES & RECIPES USED

Specific Gravity:

GLAZE TECHNIQUES

SCHEDULE

Ramp 1:

Ramp 2:

Ramp 3:

Ramp 4:

Soak:

Slow cool:

Length of firing hours:

KW used:

Cost:

PACK

Tight Moderate Loose

CONES USED CONE ACHIEVED

GLAZE RESULT

Perfect

Good

OK

Could be better

Disaster

Underfired

Bang on!

Overfired

ADDITIONAL INFO

What went wrong:

What went right:

Suggestions for next firing:

Kiln Notes
Firing Records

BISQUE　　GLAZE　　DATE: ______________

OTHER: ______________　　FIRING NO.: ______________

CLAY, GLAZES & RECIPES USED

Specific Gravity:

SCHEDULE

Ramp 1:

Ramp 2:

Ramp 3:

Ramp 4:

Soak:

Slow cool:

Length of firing hours:

KW used:

Cost:

GLAZE TECHNIQUES

PACK

Tight　　Moderate　　Loose

CONES USED　　CONE ACHIEVED

GLAZE RESULT

- Perfect
- Good
- OK
- Could be better
- Disaster

- Underfired
- Bang on!
- Overfired

ADDITIONAL INFO

What went wrong:

What went right:

Suggestions for next firing:

Kiln Notes
Firing Records

- BISQUE
- GLAZE
- OTHER: ____________

DATE: ____________

FIRING NO.: ____________

CLAY, GLAZES & RECIPES USED

Specific Gravity:

GLAZE TECHNIQUES

SCHEDULE

Ramp 1:

Ramp 2:

Ramp 3:

Ramp 4:

Soak:

Slow cool:

Length of firing hours:

KW used:

Cost:

PACK

Tight — Moderate — Loose

CONES USED

CONE ACHIEVED

GLAZE RESULT

- Perfect
- Good
- OK
- Could be better
- Disaster

- Underfired
- Bang on!
- Overfired

ADDITIONAL INFO

What went wrong:

What went right:

Suggestions for next firing:

Kiln Notes
Firing Records

BISQUE | GLAZE | DATE: ______

OTHER: ______ | FIRING NO.: ______

CLAY, GLAZES & RECIPES USED

Specific Gravity:

GLAZE TECHNIQUES

SCHEDULE

Ramp 1:

Ramp 2:

Ramp 3:

Ramp 4:

Soak:

Slow cool:

Length of firing hours:

KW used:

Cost:

PACK

Tight — Moderate — Loose

CONES USED

CONE ACHIEVED

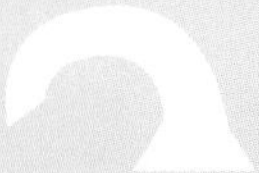

GLAZE RESULT

- Perfect
- Good
- OK
- Could be better
- Disaster

- Underfired
- Bang on!
- Overfired

ADDITIONAL INFO

What went wrong:

What went right:

Suggestions for next firing:

Kiln Notes
Firing Records

BISQUE GLAZE DATE: ____________

OTHER: ____________ FIRING NO.: ____________

CLAY, GLAZES & RECIPES USED

Specific Gravity:

GLAZE TECHNIQUES

SCHEDULE

Ramp 1:

Ramp 2:

Ramp 3:

Ramp 4:

Soak:

Slow cool:

Length of firing hours:

KW used:

Cost:

PACK

Tight Moderate Loose

CONES USED

CONE ACHIEVED

GLAZE RESULT

Perfect

Good

OK

Could be better

Disaster

Underfired

Bang on!

Overfired

ADDITIONAL INFO

What went wrong:

What went right:

Suggestions for next firing:

Kiln Notes
Firing Records

BISQUE GLAZE DATE: ______________

OTHER: ______________ FIRING NO.: ______________

CLAY, GLAZES & RECIPES USED

Specific Gravity:

GLAZE TECHNIQUES

SCHEDULE

Ramp 1:

Ramp 2:

Ramp 3:

Ramp 4:

Soak:

Slow cool:

Length of firing hours:

KW used:

Cost:

PACK

Tight — Moderate — Loose

CONES USED

CONE ACHIEVED

GLAZE RESULT

- Perfect
- Good
- OK
- Could be better
- Disaster

- Underfired
- Bang on!
- Overfired

ADDITIONAL INFO

What went wrong:

What went right:

Suggestions for next firing:

Kiln Notes
Firing Records

BISQUE GLAZE DATE: ____________

OTHER: ____________ FIRING NO.: ____________

CLAY, GLAZES & RECIPES USED

Specific Gravity:

GLAZE TECHNIQUES

SCHEDULE

Ramp 1:

Ramp 2:

Ramp 3:

Ramp 4:

Soak:

Slow cool:

Length of firing hours:

KW used:

Cost:

PACK

Tight Moderate Loose

CONES USED

CONE ACHIEVED

GLAZE RESULT

- Perfect
- Good
- OK
- Could be better
- Disaster

- Underfired
- Bang on!
- Overfired

ADDITIONAL INFO

What went wrong:

What went right:

Suggestions for next firing:

Kiln Notes
Firing Records

BISQUE GLAZE DATE: ____________

OTHER: ____________ FIRING NO.: ____________

CLAY, GLAZES & RECIPES USED

Specific Gravity:

SCHEDULE

Ramp 1:

Ramp 2:

Ramp 3:

Ramp 4:

Soak:

Slow cool:

Length of firing hours:

KW used:

Cost:

GLAZE TECHNIQUES

PACK

Tight Moderate Loose

GLAZE RESULT

Perfect

Good

OK

Could be better

Disaster

Underfired

Bang on!

Overfired

CONES USED

CONE ACHIEVED

ADDITIONAL INFO

What went wrong:

What went right:

Suggestions for next firing:

Kiln Notes Firing Records

BISQUE GLAZE DATE: ____________

OTHER: ____________ FIRING NO.: ____________

CLAY, GLAZES & RECIPES USED

Specific Gravity:

SCHEDULE

Ramp 1:

Ramp 2:

Ramp 3:

Ramp 4:

Soak:

Slow cool:

Length of firing hours:

KW used:

Cost:

GLAZE TECHNIQUES

PACK

Tight Moderate Loose

CONES USED

CONE ACHIEVED

GLAZE RESULT

Perfect

Underfired

Good

Bang on!

OK

Overfired

Could be better

Disaster

ADDITIONAL INFO

What went wrong:

What went right:

Suggestions for next firing:

Kiln Notes
Firing Records

BISQUE GLAZE DATE: ____________

OTHER: ____________ FIRING NO.: ____________

CLAY, GLAZES & RECIPES USED

Specific Gravity:

GLAZE TECHNIQUES

SCHEDULE

Ramp 1:

Ramp 2:

Ramp 3:

Ramp 4:

Soak:

Slow cool:

Length of firing hours:

KW used:

Cost:

PACK

Tight — Moderate — Loose

CONES USED

CONE ACHIEVED

GLAZE RESULT

Perfect

Good

OK

Could be better

Disaster

Underfired

Bang on!

Overfired

ADDITIONAL INFO

What went wrong:

What went right:

Suggestions for next firing:

Kiln Notes Firing Records

BISQUE GLAZE DATE:

OTHER: FIRING NO.:

CLAY, GLAZES & RECIPES USED

Specific Gravity:

SCHEDULE

Ramp 1:

Ramp 2:

Ramp 3:

Ramp 4:

Soak:

Slow cool:

Length of firing hours:

KW used:

Cost:

GLAZE TECHNIQUES

PACK

Tight Moderate Loose

CONES USED

CONE ACHIEVED

GLAZE RESULT

Perfect

Underfired

Good

Bang on!

OK

Overfired

Could be better

Disaster

ADDITIONAL INFO

What went wrong:

What went right:

Suggestions for next firing:

Kiln Notes Firing Records

BISQUE GLAZE DATE: ____________

OTHER: ____________ FIRING NO.: ____________

CLAY, GLAZES & RECIPES USED

Specific Gravity:

GLAZE TECHNIQUES

SCHEDULE

Ramp 1:

Ramp 2:

Ramp 3:

Ramp 4:

Soak:

Slow cool:

Length of firing hours:

KW used:

Cost:

PACK

Tight — Moderate — Loose

CONES USED

CONE ACHIEVED

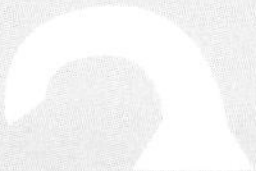

GLAZE RESULT

- Perfect
- Good
- OK
- Could be better
- Disaster

- Underfired
- Bang on!
- Overfired

ADDITIONAL INFO

What went wrong:

What went right:

Suggestions for next firing:

Kiln Notes Firing Records

BISQUE GLAZE DATE: ______

OTHER: ______ FIRING NO.: ______

CLAY, GLAZES & RECIPES USED

Specific Gravity:

SCHEDULE

Ramp 1:

Ramp 2:

Ramp 3:

Ramp 4:

Soak:

Slow cool:

GLAZE TECHNIQUES

Length of firing hours:

KW used:

Cost:

PACK

Tight Moderate Loose

GLAZE RESULT

Perfect

Good

OK

Could be better

Disaster

Underfired

Bang on!

Overfired

CONES USED

CONE ACHIEVED

ADDITIONAL INFO

What went wrong:

What went right:

Suggestions for next firing:

Kiln Notes
Firing Records

BISQUE GLAZE DATE: ____________

OTHER: ____________ FIRING NO.: ____________

CLAY, GLAZES & RECIPES USED

Specific Gravity:

SCHEDULE

Ramp 1:

Ramp 2:

Ramp 3:

Ramp 4:

Soak:

Slow cool:

Length of firing hours:

KW used:

Cost:

GLAZE TECHNIQUES

PACK

Tight — Moderate — Loose

GLAZE RESULT

- Perfect
- Good
- OK
- Could be better
- Disaster

- Underfired
- Bang on!
- Overfired

CONES USED

CONE ACHIEVED

ADDITIONAL INFO

What went wrong:

What went right:

Suggestions for next firing:

Kiln Notes Firing Records

BISQUE GLAZE DATE: ______

OTHER: ______ FIRING NO.: ______

CLAY, GLAZES & RECIPES USED

Specific Gravity:

SCHEDULE

Ramp 1:

Ramp 2:

Ramp 3:

Ramp 4:

Soak:

Slow cool:

GLAZE TECHNIQUES

Length of firing hours:

KW used:

Cost:

PACK

Tight Moderate Loose

CONES USED CONE ACHIEVED

GLAZE RESULT

Perfect Underfired

Good Bang on!

OK Overfired

Could be better

Disaster

ADDITIONAL INFO

What went wrong: What went right: Suggestions for next firing:

Kiln Notes
Firing Records

BISQUE GLAZE DATE: ____________

OTHER: ____________ FIRING NO.: ____________

CLAY, GLAZES & RECIPES USED

Specific Gravity:

GLAZE TECHNIQUES

SCHEDULE

Ramp 1:

Ramp 2:

Ramp 3:

Ramp 4:

Soak:

Slow cool:

Length of firing hours:

KW used:

Cost:

PACK

Tight Moderate Loose

CONES USED

CONE ACHIEVED

GLAZE RESULT

Perfect

Good

OK

Could be better

Disaster

Underfired

Bang on!

Overfired

ADDITIONAL INFO

What went wrong:

What went right:

Suggestions for next firing:

Kiln Notes
Firing Records

BISQUE   GLAZE   DATE: ______

OTHER: ______   FIRING NO.: ______

CLAY, GLAZES & RECIPES USED

Specific Gravity:

GLAZE TECHNIQUES

SCHEDULE

Ramp 1:

Ramp 2:

Ramp 3:

Ramp 4:

Soak:

Slow cool:

Length of firing hours:

KW used:

Cost:

PACK

Tight   Moderate   Loose

CONES USED

CONE ACHIEVED

GLAZE RESULT

Perfect   Underfired

Good   Bang on!

OK   Overfired

Could be better

Disaster

ADDITIONAL INFO

What went wrong:

What went right:

Suggestions for next firing:

Kiln Notes
Firing Records

BISQUE GLAZE DATE: ______

OTHER: ______ FIRING NO.: ______

CLAY, GLAZES & RECIPES USED

Specific Gravity:

SCHEDULE

Ramp 1:

Ramp 2:

Ramp 3:

Ramp 4:

Soak:

Slow cool:

Length of firing hours:

KW used:

Cost:

GLAZE TECHNIQUES

PACK

Tight Moderate Loose

CONES USED

CONE ACHIEVED

GLAZE RESULT

- Perfect
- Good
- OK
- Could be better
- Disaster

- Underfired
- Bang on!
- Overfired

ADDITIONAL INFO

What went wrong:

What went right:

Suggestions for next firing:

Kiln Notes Firing Records

BISQUE GLAZE DATE: ______

OTHER: ______ FIRING NO.: ______

CLAY, GLAZES & RECIPES USED

Specific Gravity:

GLAZE TECHNIQUES

SCHEDULE

Ramp 1:

Ramp 2:

Ramp 3:

Ramp 4:

Soak:

Slow cool:

Length of firing hours:

KW used:

Cost:

PACK

Tight Moderate Loose

CONES USED

CONE ACHIEVED

GLAZE RESULT

Perfect

Good

OK

Could be better

Disaster

Underfired

Bang on!

Overfired

ADDITIONAL INFO

What went wrong:

What went right:

Suggestions for next firing:

Kiln Notes
Firing Records

BISQUE GLAZE DATE: ____________

OTHER: ____________ FIRING NO.: ____________

CLAY, GLAZES & RECIPES USED

Specific Gravity:

SCHEDULE

Ramp 1:

Ramp 2:

Ramp 3:

Ramp 4:

Soak:

Slow cool:

Length of firing hours:

KW used:

Cost:

GLAZE TECHNIQUES

PACK

Tight Moderate Loose

GLAZE RESULT

- Perfect
- Good
- OK
- Could be better
- Disaster

- Underfired
- Bang on!
- Overfired

CONES USED

CONE ACHIEVED

ADDITIONAL INFO

What went wrong:

What went right:

Suggestions for next firing:

Kiln Notes
Firing Records

BISQUE GLAZE DATE: ____________

OTHER: ____________ FIRING NO.: ____________

CLAY, GLAZES & RECIPES USED

Specific Gravity:

GLAZE TECHNIQUES

SCHEDULE

Ramp 1:

Ramp 2:

Ramp 3:

Ramp 4:

Soak:

Slow cool:

Length of firing hours:

KW used:

Cost:

PACK

Tight Moderate Loose

CONES USED

CONE ACHIEVED

GLAZE RESULT

Perfect

Good

OK

Could be better

Disaster

Underfired

Bang on!

Overfired

ADDITIONAL INFO

What went wrong:

What went right:

Suggestions for next firing:

Kiln Notes
Firing Records

BISQUE   GLAZE   DATE: ____________

OTHER: ____________   FIRING NO.: ____________

CLAY, GLAZES & RECIPES USED

Specific Gravity:

SCHEDULE

Ramp 1:

Ramp 2:

Ramp 3:

Ramp 4:

Soak:

Slow cool:

Length of firing hours:

KW used:

Cost:

GLAZE TECHNIQUES

PACK

Tight   Moderate   Loose

GLAZE RESULT

Perfect

Good

OK

Could be better

Disaster

Underfired

Bang on!

Overfired

CONES USED

CONE ACHIEVED

ADDITIONAL INFO

What went wrong:

What went right:

Suggestions for next firing:

My Glaze Recipes

Write down your favorite glaze recipes or combinations here.

My Glaze Recipes

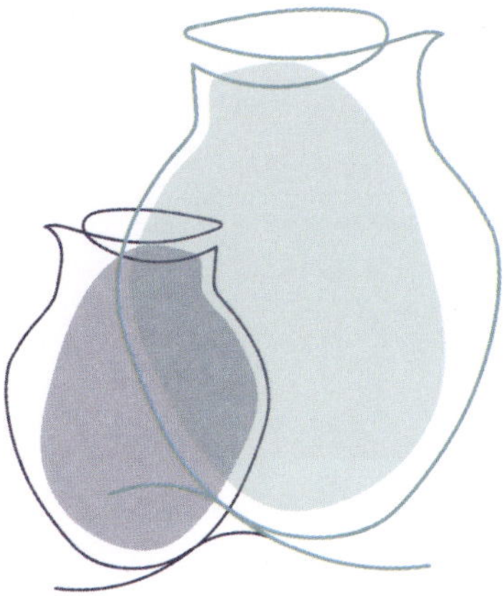

My Glaze Recipes

My Glaze Recipes

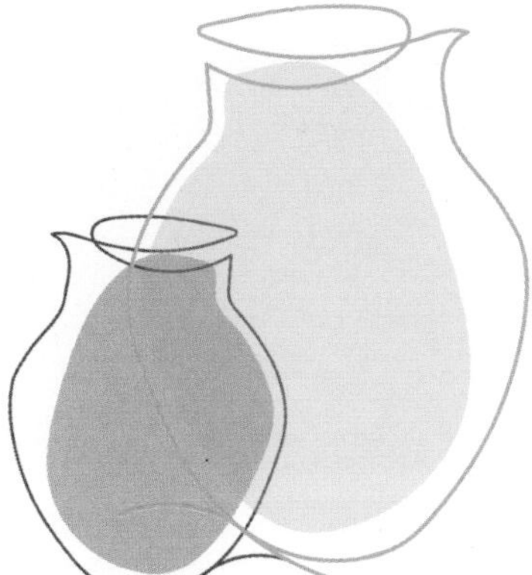

My Glaze Recipes

My Glaze Recipes

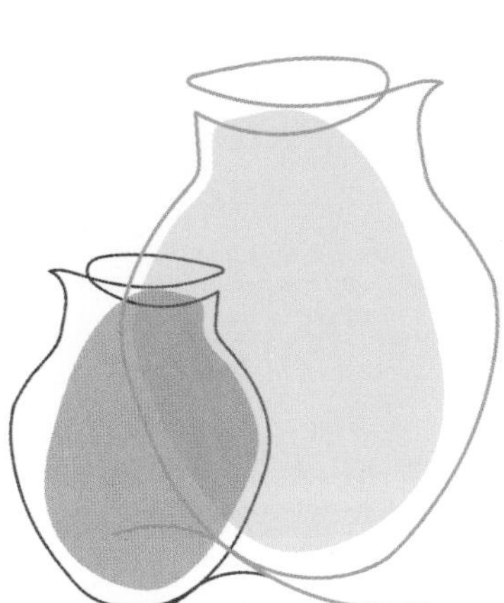

My Glaze Recipes

My Glaze Recipes

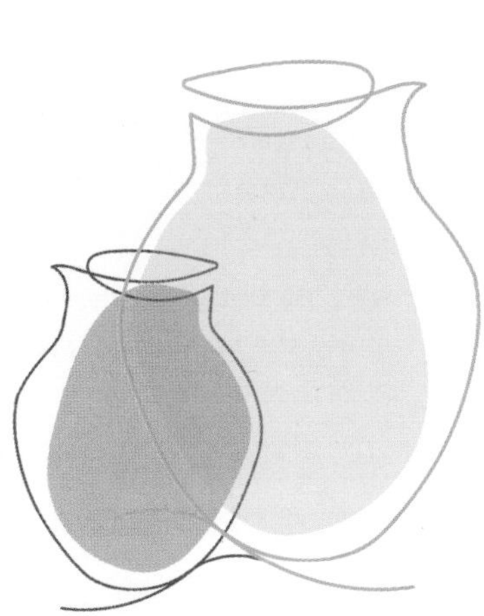

Firing Glossary

Heat work: Heat work is the combined effect of heat over a period of time. As potters, we are much more concerned with heat work versus purely temperature. It takes the accumulation of heat over a period of time for clay and glaze to absorb the heat work it needs to become ceramic. A bit like in your home oven, we can either cook something at a high temperature for a shorter period of time or at a low temperature for a longer period of time.

Top temperature: This is the highest temperature the kiln will reach during your firing.

Schedule: This is the temperature you want your kiln to get to and how fast you want it to get there. It can be slow, medium or fast on a manual or gas kiln, or it may be done in ramps (see below for explanation of ramp) on a digital controller.

Ramp: This refers to how many degrees per hour your kiln will heat up as programmed into its digital controller (e.g., 212°F [100°C] per hour).

Soak: This refers to holding the top temperature for a period of time (normally in 15-minute increments) to help even out the heat work throughout the kiln. The middle of a kiln tends to be hottest, with cooler shelves at the bottom. You may want to add a soak to a glaze firing to even out the temperature, making sure all shelves reach the same cone. Or pack the kiln more heavily in the middle. This is especially useful in larger kilns. For example: For my large 117-liter kiln, I add a 15-minute soak at 2183°F (1195°C) for my cone 6 firings. This evens out the temperature throughout my kiln before the firing then climbs to its final temperature of 2232°F (1222°C).

Vitrification (or maturity): Clay and glaze remain porous and relatively weak until they are fired to their vitrification temperature. You need your pots to be glazed, fired and vitrified or fired to maturity in order to hold your coffee. It is important to note the firing temperature of your clay and glazes when you buy them, as this will inform the temperature the kiln must be fired to. Your clay and glaze temperatures must always be within the same firing range.

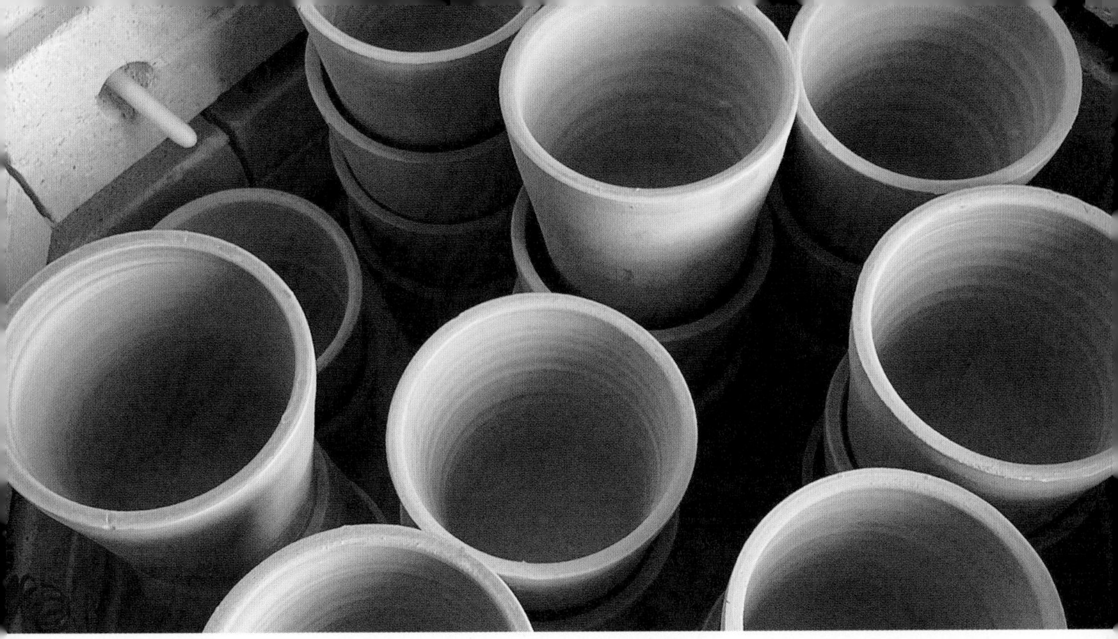

Element wear: Elements generally last between 50 to 150 firings (average being 100), but this varies depending on things such as the temperature you fire to and the glazes you use. Hotter firings wear elements quicker. A potter using cone 10 porcelain may need to change their elements sooner than a potter using cone 6 stoneware.

As the elements in a kiln age, your firings will likely take longer, and it will take more energy to pass a current through the element. Eventually, they might not even be able to reach temperature at all!

The longer your firings take and the longer elements spend at a higher temperature, the more they wear. Certain materials in glaze recipes will also wear your elements more than others. Keeping peepholes open until 1112°F (600°C) can help elements last longer as this allows corrosive vapors to escape. Having a downdraft vent will help pull vapors out of the kiln and away from elements, making them last longer.

Using cones and keeping accurate notes of how long your firings are taking will help you predict when you need to change your elements—which is much better than getting caught out a week before your next craft market! Other parts of a kiln can wear out too such as the thermocouple and relays. Keeping a record of how many firings your kiln has done will help you maintain your kiln's health and ensure it keeps firing consistently.

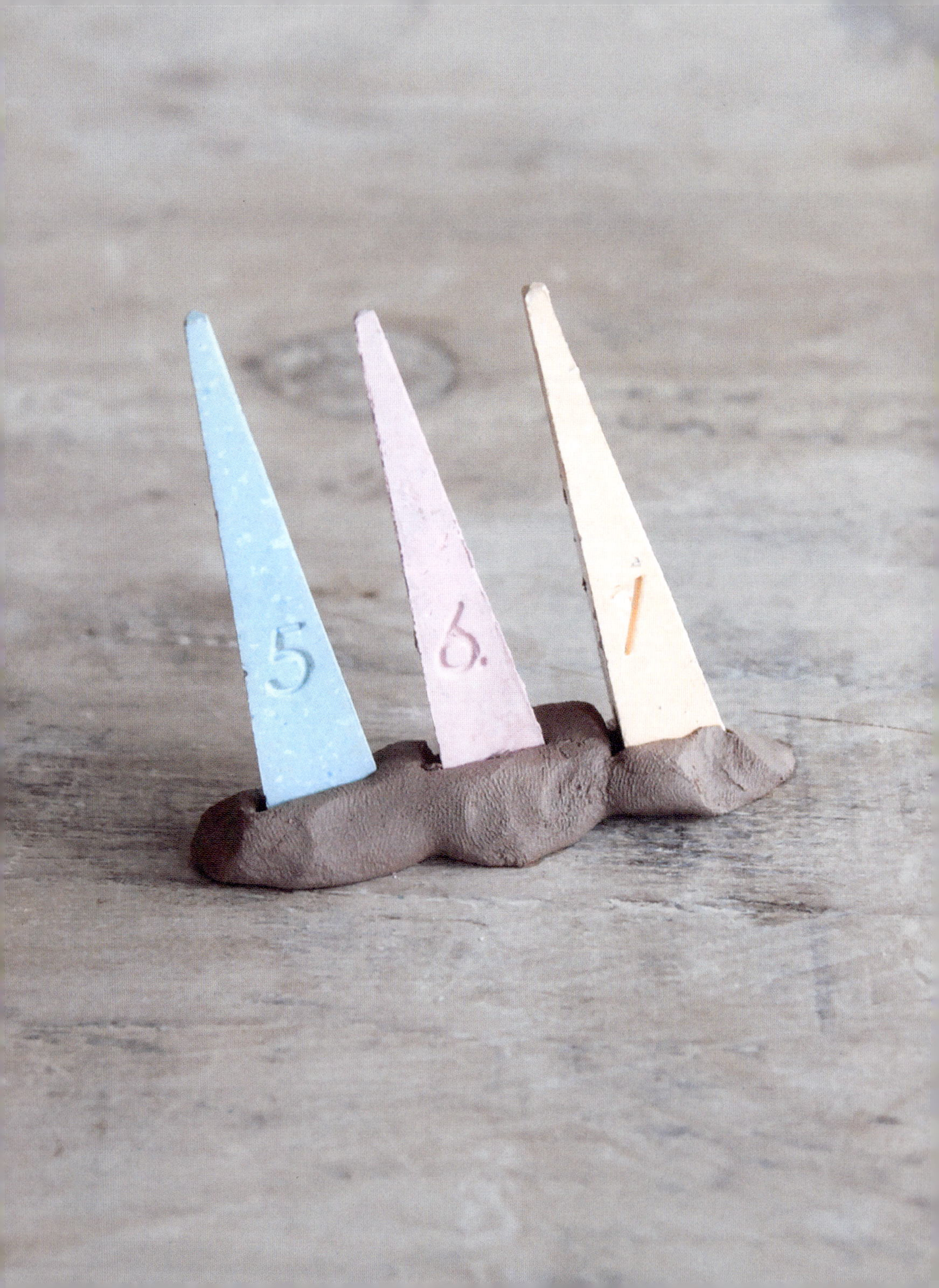
5
6.
7

What Are Cones?

Cones are made of ceramic material just like your clay and glazes. They are designed to melt and bend at very specific temperatures according to how much heat work they have been exposed to during a firing.

In most modern digital kilns, temperature is measured by the kiln's thermocouple at a single spot in the kiln and is displayed in Fahrenheit or Celsius on your kiln's digital controller.

As we know, heat work takes things a step further and is the accumulative effect that temperature has *over a period of time*. **Pyrometric cones are the only real way of reading the heat work your pottery has absorbed.** They may sound technical, but they are a useful little tool for all potters.

Some clays and glazes have a wide firing range, while others need much more accuracy to get the desired results. So many issues we encounter as potters have to do with what goes on inside our kiln (e.g., if your glazes ran during a firing, this could mean the glaze was applied too thickly or your kiln overfired). Cones help us understand if we have underfired, overfired or reached our desired heat work. If the cones look good, we can rule out the firing as an issue. By using cones in all our glaze firings, accurately recording our processes and results, we can identify issues and replicate good results next time.

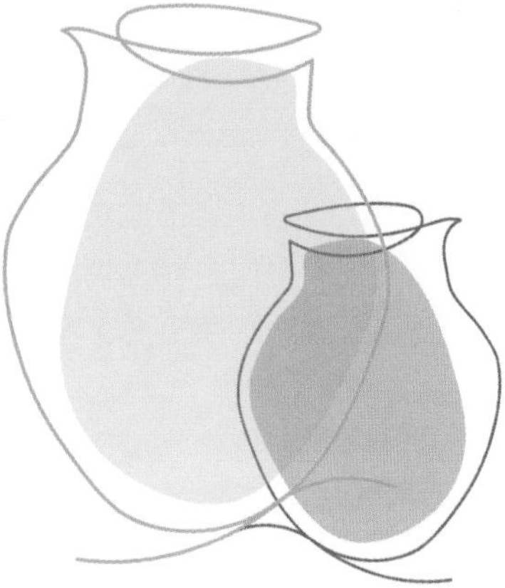

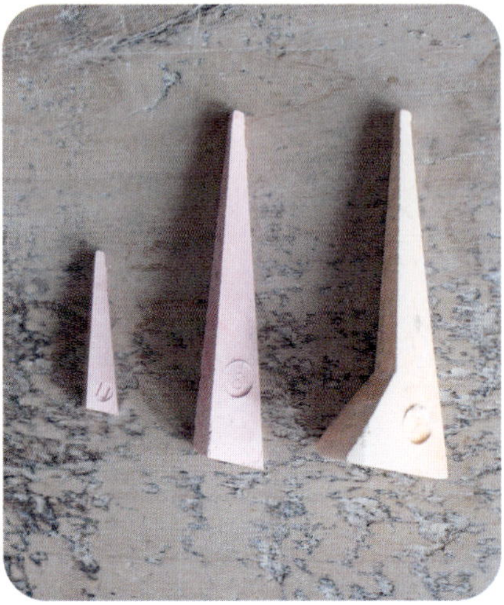

Small cone on the left compared to a large standard cone in the middle and a self-supporting cone on the right.

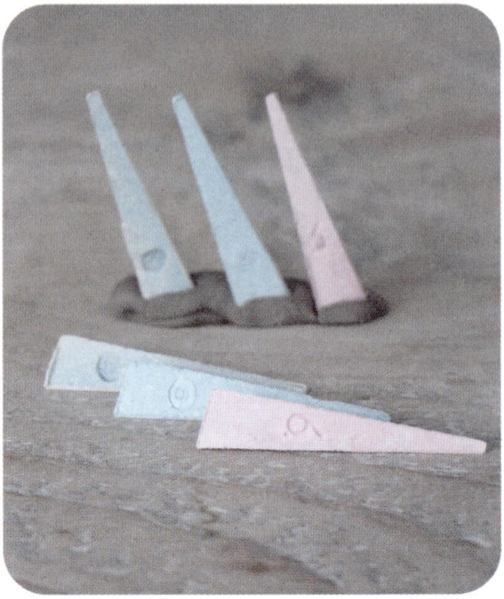

A cone pack consisting of cone 4, cone 5 and cone 6.

Types of Cones

Cones range from cone 022 very low temperature to cone 14 very high temperature. See cone charts on pages 184 and 185 for equivalent temperatures.

Small Cones and Bar Cones: These are used in a kiln sitter in a manual kiln. These bend and drop the lever to shut off the kiln when it has reached temperature. *They cannot be used interchangeably with standard or self-supporting cones.* **Note:** I won't be referring to these throughout this book as they bend differently than standard or self-supporting cones. If you use a manual kiln, I still recommend using standard or self-supporting cones to record the heat work in your firings.

Standard Cones: These are referred to as witness cones, as they are literally "witnessing the firing." These can be stood in small sausages of clay to create a cone pack. (See page 175 to learn how to make a cone pack.)

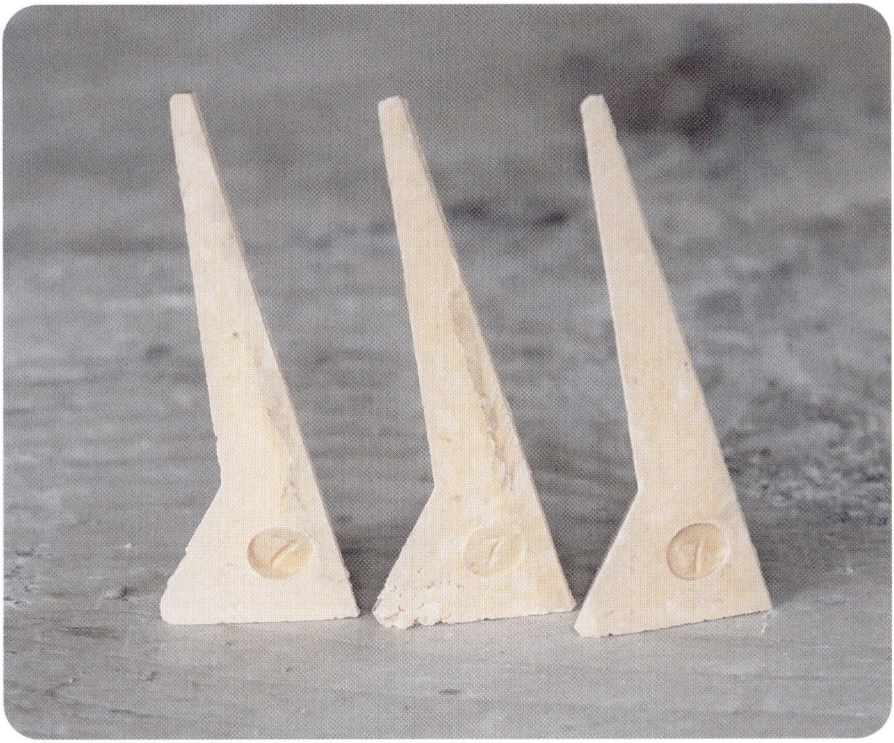

Three cone 7 self-supporting cones.

Self-Supporting Cones: These are also referred to as witness cones, but they have a small additional triangle at the base, which means they stand up on their own and do not need clay sausages. They are a little more expensive, but you can always be sure they are at the correct angle, and they don't need to be placed into clay.

I will be referring to both standard and self-supporting cones interchangeably throughout this notebook.

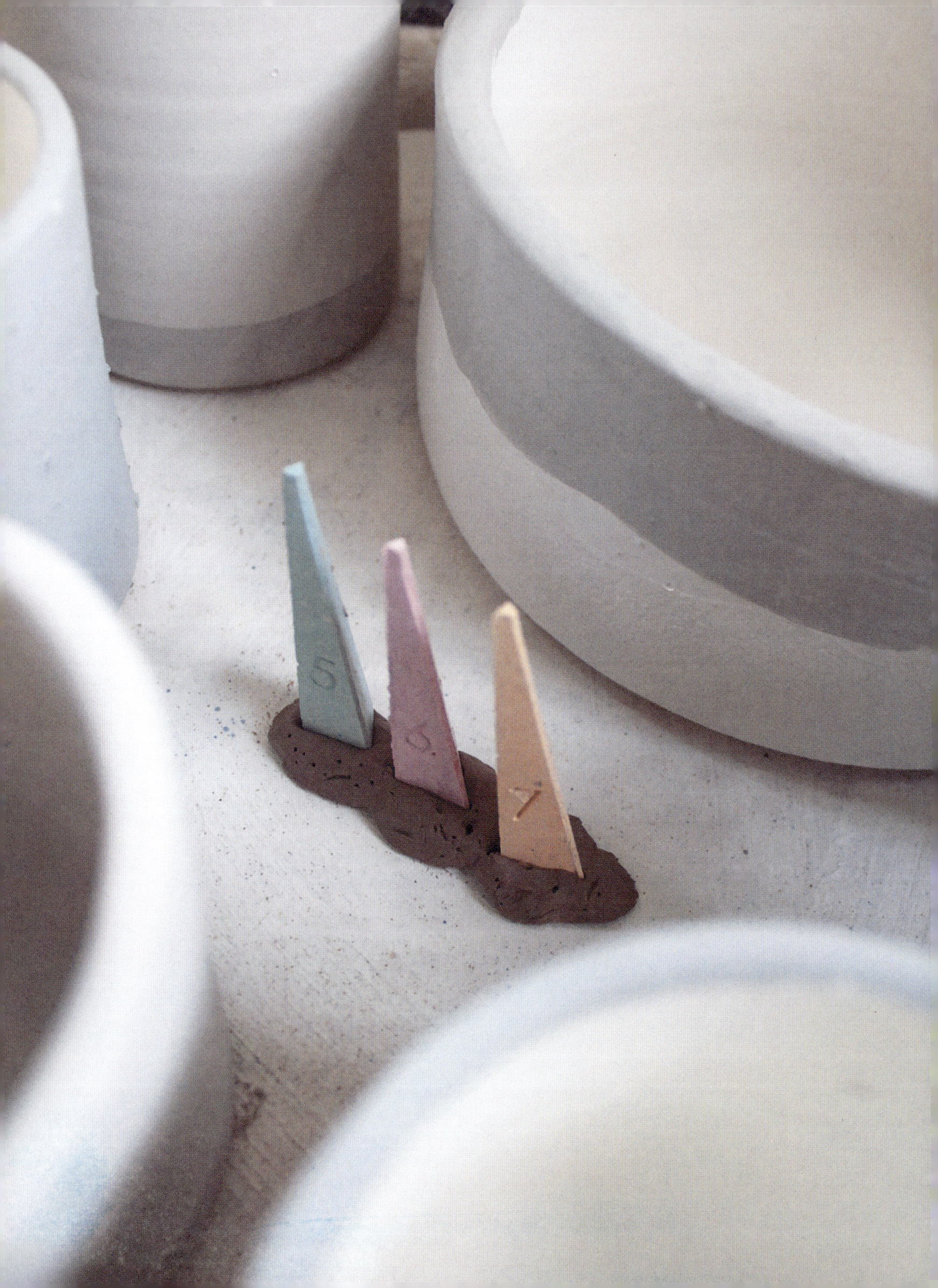
5
7

How to Use Cones

Always use the cones that match the temperature of the glazes and clay you are using.

Be careful: Cone 06 and cone 6 are very different!

- A cone 6 will bend at around 2232°F (1222°C) depending upon the speed of the firing. This is a mid-fire or low stoneware.
- Cone 06 will bend at around 1830°F (999°C), so it is for low-fire or earthenware.

To use cones, you normally use three. This is called a "cone pack." For a cone 6 firing you would use cone 5, cone 6 and cone 7.

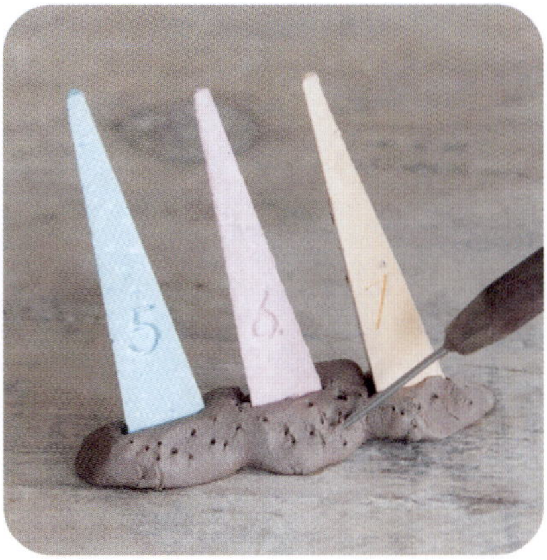

The above image is a 6 cone pack.

- **The Guide Cone** (cone 5) is the one to the left.
- **The Target Cone** (cone 6) is the middle cone—the heat work or cone you are aiming for.
- **The Guard Cone** (cone 7) is the one to the right.

Making a Cone Pack

You can put standard large cones into a little sausage of soft clay (no bigger than the thickness of a pencil). Gently push the cone all the way through the clay until the base is touching the surface of the table. This ensures they are sitting at the correct angle, which is determined by the slope of the base. You can squash the clay back around the base to keep them in place if need be.

Poke the clay with a needle tool (as shown in the image above) to ensure any water quickly escapes in the firing and avoids explosions. You can wait until the clay is bone dry before putting it in the kiln. I normally make a whole bunch of cone packs in advance so they are ready and dry when I need them.

If you are using specifically made cone holders, like the one on page 183, make sure the falling face always goes next to the dot. (If you stand a cone on a table, the falling face is the direction the cone falls.)

NOTE

If you try to stand a standard large cone up on its own, it will fall over. This is due to the specific angle of the base which, with the help of gravity, ensures the cone bends correctly. Ensuring the cones are at the correct angle is important. If you stand a cone on a table the falling face is the direction the cone falls.

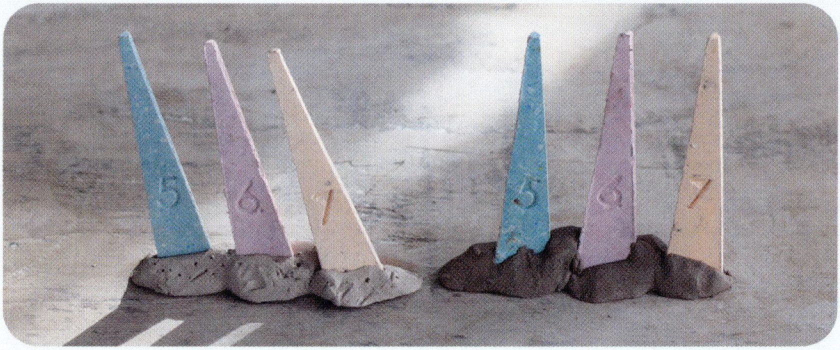

The cone pack on the left is correct; note the slight lean to the left. The cone pack on the right is incorrect; note they are pointing straight up and won't bend properly in the firing.

Cone Placement

With gas and wood firings, potters put cone packs near the vents or peepholes so they can be observed during the firing. This must be done wearing welding goggles or there is a risk to the eyesight. In my experience with electric kilns, and certainly those new to firing their own kilns, it is very awkward to get cones in the correct position and difficult to see them when the kiln is white hot. It's best to look at cones retrospectively—that is *after* the firing.

We need to put the cones far enough away from our work so when they bend they don't stick to it. The middle of a kiln shelf is best and is the most accurate representation of heat work. For larger kilns, it's best to put a cone pack on the bottom, middle and top shelf. For smaller kilns, you shouldn't get a lot of difference in heat work between shelves, so one cone pack on the middle shelf will normally suffice.

NOTE

Be careful when handling cones as they are fragile and can break easily. Hold the ends and twist them apart. Or hold one on the end, flush to the edge of a table and push down on the other. See the image below for reference.

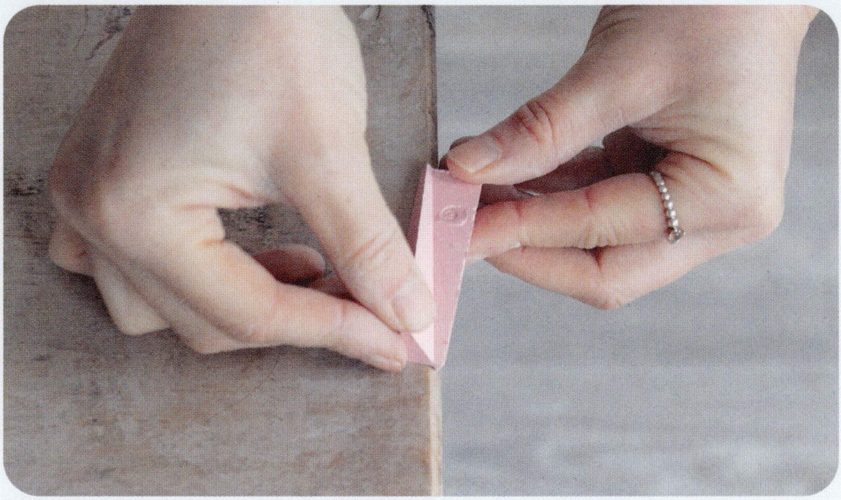

Good to know:

- Cones lose their color after they've been fired and turn white. This is so that even if the cones haven't bent, you know they've been used.
- You can only use cones once.
- Specifically made cone holders, like the one on page 183, are single use. As a reminder, the falling face always goes next to the dot.

How to Read Cones (Have You Had a Successful Firing?)

You know you have the perfect heat work when the guide cone (left) melts first and likely melts completely. The target cone (middle) will bend over next in an elegant arc. The guard cone (right) will remain straight or only start to bend slightly.

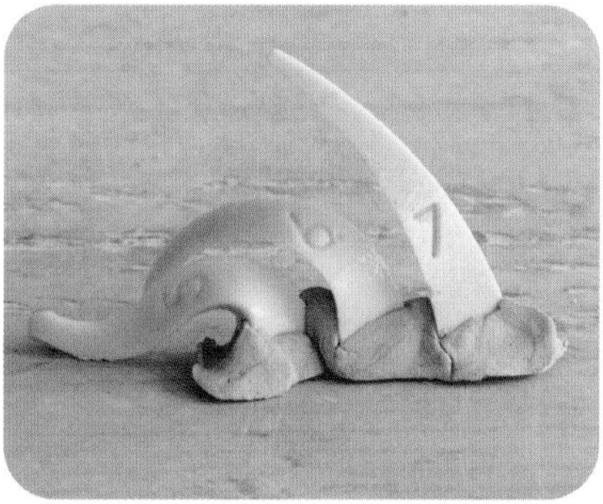

This firing has reached a perfect cone 6.

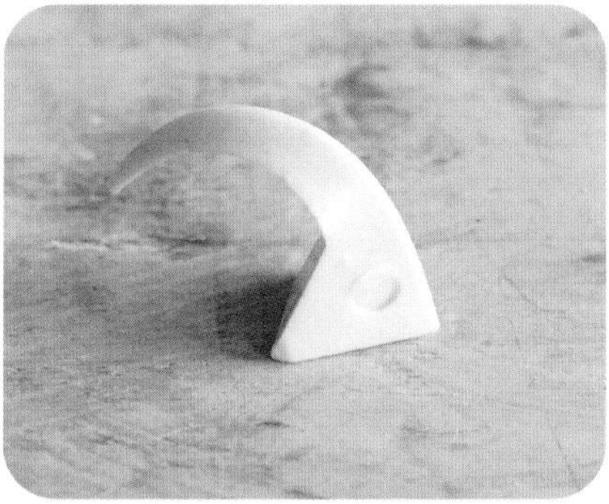

Contrary to popular belief, the tip does not have to touch the kiln shelf.

Example of Overfiring

Image 1 shows that the firing was too hot. These cones absorbed too much heat work. The glazes and clay in this kiln load may show signs of overfiring (e.g., running, blistering, bloating, etc.).

How to fix: I'll need to reduce the temperature of the kiln next time, speed up the firing, remove the soak or a combination of all three.

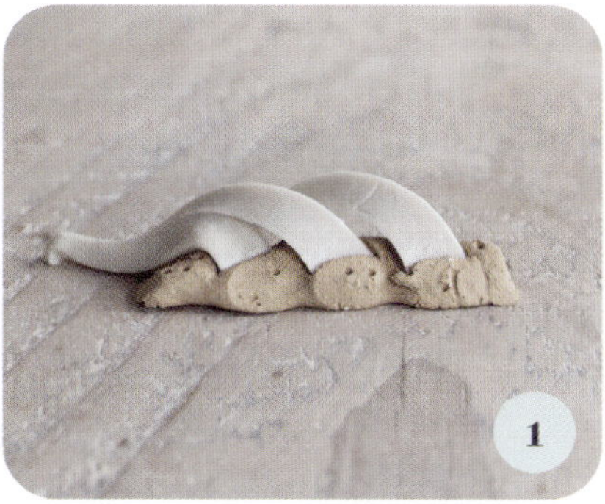

Overfiring: All the cones, including the guard cone, have melted and bent all the way over.

Example of Underfiring

Image 2 shows the work on this shelf didn't quite reach the temperature I wanted. This tells me my pottery and cones did not absorb enough heat work to vitrify cone 6 clay and glazes.

How to fix: I'll need to increase the top temperature of my firing schedule, slow down the firing or add a soak onto the end of my firing next time.

The key is in the tip of the cone. If the tip is still angled up, it hasn't quite reached the temperature range required. Once the tip is pointing down, the melt of the cone is quite rapid.

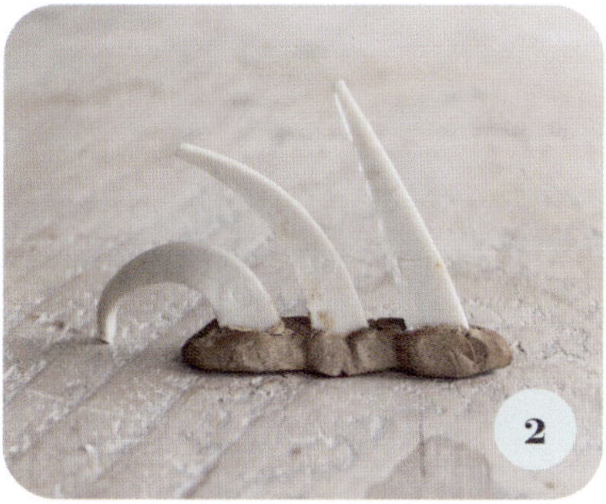

Underfiring: Note that the middle cone, cone 6 which is the target cone, has only bent a little bit. This was more like a cone 5.5 firing.

PRO TIP

The difference between the bend in these two cones represents only about 35 degrees Fahrenheit (19 degrees Celsius)!

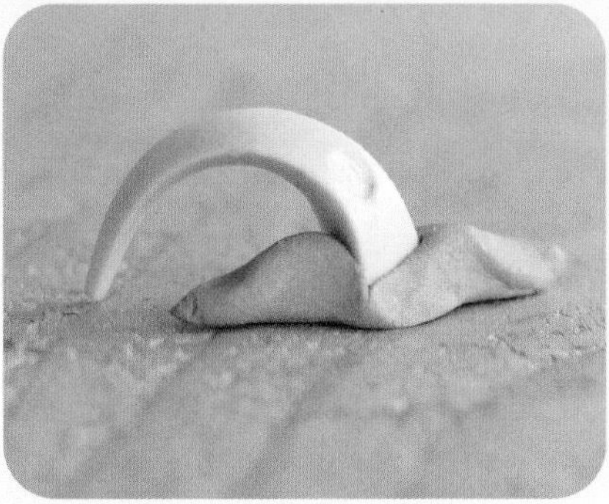

Note the tip is touching the table.

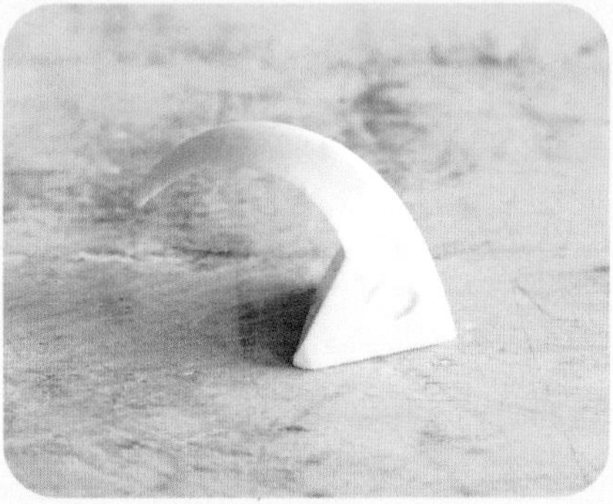

Note the tip is pointing down but hasn't quite touched the table. As long as your tip is angled down you are within the target cone tolerance.

You will need to put cones in all glaze firings to ensure your adjustments have had the desired effect and maintain consistency. Don't forget to record what you did and your results straight away in your notebook!

GOOD TO KNOW

You don't need to put cones in all your bisque firings. Our goal is not to vitrify our pottery during bisque firings, so it's not as critical to ensure we have reached a specific temperature/amount of heat work.

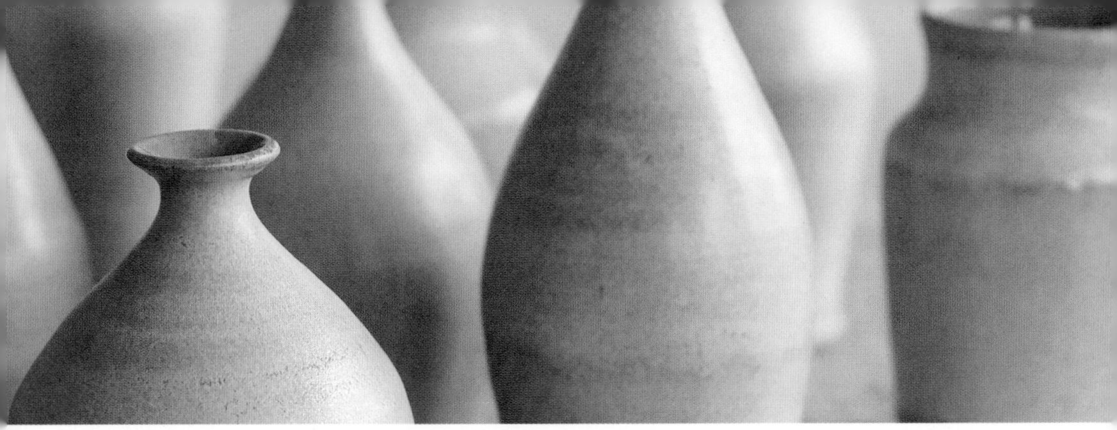

Variables that can affect heat work:

- The peak temperature the kiln reached.
- The period of time the work is in the kiln.
- The amount of work in the firing. Tightly packed kilns take longer to heat up so the time variable needs to increase, but the top temperature will need to be adjusted lower to reach the required heat work value.
- How the shelves are placed. Ensuring shelves are well distributed throughout the kiln will help it to heat evenly.
- Some kilns tend to be hotter in the middle. Stacking the middle of the kiln more densely with work will help to even out the heat work.

Glaze only starts to melt in the final 212°F (100°C) of a firing. Note the Heating Rate on the cone chart on pages 184 to 185. This refers to the ramp used ONLY during the final 212°F (100°C) of the firing.

Slower firings can give more interesting glaze results as it has given the glazes more time to "mature" (when all the ingredients in the glaze melt and mingle together). Remember a slower firing will use more energy.

To get the benefit of a slow firing while also using less energy, it's possible to use a relatively fast-firing schedule and then slow the ramp in the final 212°F (100°C). Alternatively, you could add a soak period onto the end of your firing. A 15- to 20-minute hold is roughly equal to one cone's worth of heat. You may need to lower the top temperature to compensate for the additional time, but not always.

To recap:

- Putting cones in every glaze firing will help you best understand how your kiln is firing.
- Always refer to the cone chart on pages 184 and 185 to make sure you are using the correct cones for your glazes.
- Cones will always bend in a consistent way in reaction to the heat and time they are exposed to in the kiln. From batch to batch they are carefully tested by the manufacturer for accuracy.
- Commercial glazes and clays will always have the cone or firing temperature displayed on the packaging.

A quick note about glaze and food safety:

One major way (but not the only way) to ensure pottery is safe to use with food is to make sure the clay and glazes you use become fully matured (or cooked) during the firing. This means colorant oxides become chemically bound into the glaze and are unlikely to leach out. Keeping accurate notes and using cones in your firings to ensure you reached the desired heat work are two due diligences that potters can employ.

Other ways include but are not exclusive to:

- Only use commercial glazes labeled as lead free and food or dinnerware safe.
- Do not use glaze with lots of texture for surfaces which come in contact with food.
- If you make your own glazes, it's best to steer clear of toxic ingredients such as lead, cadmium, barium and lithium.
- Use color oxides in low percentages (<3%).

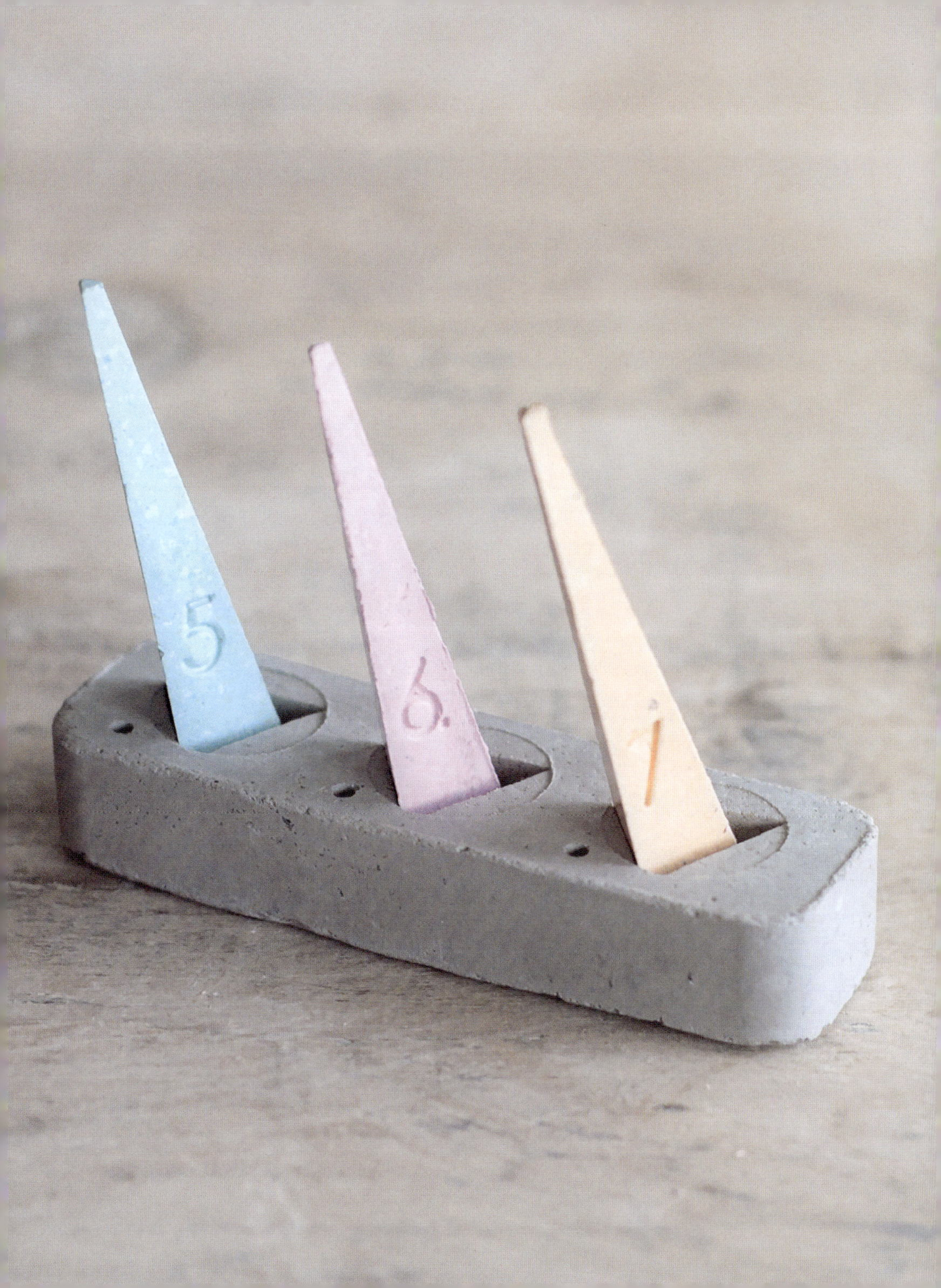
5
6.
7

Cones Charts

Temperature Equivalents (°F) For Orton Pyrometric Cones				
	Self-supporting cones		Large Regular Cones	
Heating Rate used	108°F/hr	270°F/hr	108°F/hr	270°F/hr
How fast was your firing rate	Medium	Fast	Medium	Fast
Cone Number				
022	1087	1094	N/A	N/A
021	1112	1143	N/A	N/A
020	1159	1180	N/A	N/A
019	1252	1283	1249	1279
018	1319	1353	1314	1350
017	1360	1405	1357	1402
016	1422	1465	1416	1461
015	1456	1504	1450	1501
014	1485	1540	1485	1537
013	1539	1582	1539	1578
012	1582	1620	1576	1616
011	1607	1641	1603	1638
010	1657	1679	1648	1675
09	1688	1706	1683	1702
08	1728	1753	1728	1749
07	1789	1809	1783	1805
06	1828	1855	1823	1852
05½	1859	1877	1854	1873
05	1888	1911	1886	1915
04	1945	1971	1940	1958
03	1987	2019	1987	2014
02	2016	2052	2014	2048
01	2046	2080	2043	2079
1	2079	2109	2077	2109
2	2088	2127	2088	2124
3	2106	2138	2106	2134
4	2124	2161	2120	2158
5	2167	2205	2163	2201
5½	2197	2237	N/A	N/A
6	2231	2269	2228	2266
7	2262	2295	2259	2291
8	2280	2320	2277	2316
9	2300	2336	2295	2332
10	2345	2381	2340	2377
11	2361	2399	2359	2394
12	2383	2419	2379	2415
13	2428	2458	2410	2455
14	2489	2523	2530	2491

Temperature Equivalents (°C) For Orton Pyrometric Cones				
	Self-supporting cones		**Large Regular Cones**	
Heating Rate used	60°C/hr	150°C/hr	60°C/hr	150°C/hr
How fast was your firing rate	Medium	Fast	Medium	Fast
Cone Number				
022	586	590	N/A	N/A
021	600	617	N/A	N/A
020	626	638	N/A	N/A
019	678	695	676	693
018	715	734	712	732
017	738	763	736	761
016	772	796	769	794
015	791	818	788	816
014	807	838	807	836
013	837	861	837	859
012	861	882	858	880
011	875	894	873	892
010	903	915	898	913
09	920	930	917	928
08	942	956	942	954
07	976	987	973	985
06	998	1013	995	1011
05½	1015	1025	1012	1023
05	1031	1044	1030	1046
04	1063	1077	1060	1070
03	1086	1104	1086	1101
02	1102	1122	1101	1120
01	1119	1138	1117	1137
1	1137	1154	1136	1154
2	1142	1164	1142	1162
3	1152	1170	1152	1168
4	1162	1183	1160	1181
5	1186	1207	1184	1205
5½	1203	1225	N/A	N/A
6	1222	1243	1220	1241
7	1239	1257	1237	1255
8	1249	1271	1247	1269
9	1260	1280	1257	1278
10	1285	1305	1282	1303
11	1294	1315	1293	1312
12	1306	1326	1304	1324
13	1331	1348	1321	1346
14	1365	1384	1388	1366

Kiln Schedules

There are no one-size-fits-all kiln schedules. The heat work achieved in your firing relies on many variables. You will need to test some schedules out to determine the correct firing for your work.

Most firings in an electric kiln (except for luster and decal) take between 8 to 12 hours and then at least an additional 24 hours to cool down depending on the size of the kiln. Small kilns tend to cool faster.

For safety reasons, it is always best to wait until it has cooled to room temperature before unloading.

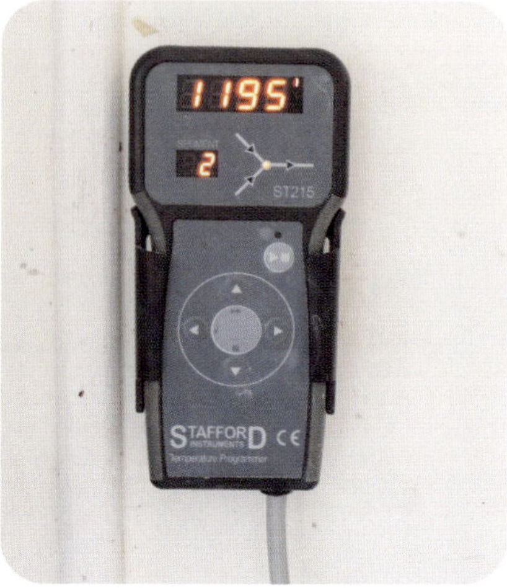

It is to be expected to need to test a new kiln or any new glazes to find the best schedule for your desired result.

New kilns come with a manual and recommended firing schedules. If you bought your kiln secondhand or don't have the manual, here are some suggested general schedules for kilns with digital controllers. These should be used as a starting point as all kilns fire slightly differently. Even kilns of the same brand and of a similar size can vary. You may need to adjust these schedules depending on the clay and glaze you are using and your desired results. For example, my small 45-liter kiln is so well insulated, it achieves a cone 6 firing with a top temperature of 2183°F (1195°C).

NOTE

A slower firing schedule with a lower top temperature can have similar heat work as a fast schedule at a higher top temperature. Which works best for your work depends on the type of kiln you use, the clay, glazes, how the kiln is packed and the aesthetic you are looking for.

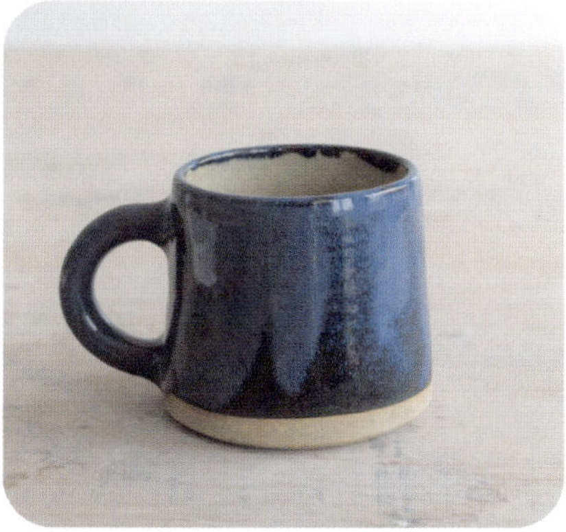

Fast firing

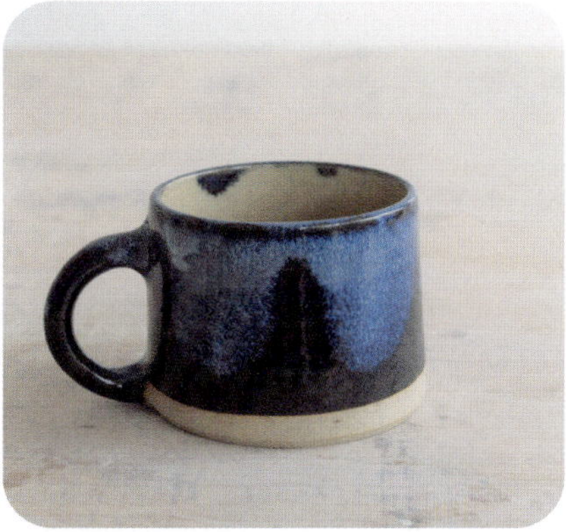

Slow firing

For example, both of these pots were fired in my kiln in two separate firings on different schedules with different top temperatures and ramps. They are the same glaze and the same clay. They have produced a similar result. Both are vitrified, but the glaze on the right (in the slower firing) has a slightly better result (in my opinion) as the glaze ingredients have had more time to mingle and mature.

The mug on the left

- **Ramp 1:** 212°F (100°C) per hour to 572°F (300°C)
- **Ramp 2:** 392°F (200°C) per hour to 2264°F (1240°C) (top temp)
- No soak
- 7¾ hours approximately (depending on the age of your elements—see page 169)

The mug on the right

- **Ramp 1:** 212°F (100°C) per hour to 572°F (300°C)
- **Ramp 2:** 392°F (200°C) per hour to 2057°F (1125°C)
- **Ramp 3:** 140°F (60°C) per hour to 2228°F (1220°C) (top temp)
- 20-minute soak
- 9 hours approximately (depending on the age of your elements—see page 169)

Kiln Schedule Examples

Ghost Firing

This is a firing for a new kiln or a new set of elements. This includes furniture—shelves and stilts—but without any pottery. This helps oxidize the elements and protect them from fumes and water vapor damage during future firings. **Note:** Please refer to your kiln manufacturer's manual in the first instance as recommended ghost firings can vary by brand.

- **Ramp 1:** 176°F (80°C) per hour to 1112°F (600°C)
- **Ramp 2:** 302°F (150°C) per hour to 1922°F (1050°C)
- 1½-hour soak
- Vents open throughout

Bisque

For bisque firings, you want to take it slow as there may be residual moisture left in the clay. With the bisque firing we do not need to vitrify the clay, but only make it less brittle so it is easier to handle while glazing. Normally, potters will bisque to between 1652 and 1940°F (900 and 1060°C).

- **Ramp 1:** 176°F (80°C) per hour to 1112°F (600°C)
- **Ramp 2:** 302°F (150°C) per hour to 1922°F (1050°C)
- 15-minute soak
- Vents open throughout

Earthenware Glaze Firing

- **Ramp 1:** 212°F (100°C) per hour to 572°F (300°C)
- **Ramp 2:** 302°F (150°C) per hour to 2102°F (1150°C)
- No soak
- Close vents at 1112°F (600°C)

Fast Stoneware Glaze Firing—Cone 6

- **Ramp 1:** 212°F (100°C) per hour to 572°F (300°C)
- **Ramp 2:** 302°F (150°C) per hour to 2228°F (1220°C)
- 15-minute soak
- Close vents at 1112°F (600°C)

Slow Stoneware Glaze Firing—Cone 8

- **Ramp 1:** 212°F (100°C) per hour to 572°F (300°C)
- **Ramp 2:** 302°F (150°C) per hour to 2050°F (1121°C)
- **Ramp 3:** 140°F (60°C) per hour to 2246°F (1230°C)
- 15-minute soak
- Close vents at 1112°F (600°C)

Slow Cool Schedule for Crystalline Glazes

Add this ramp to the end of either a Fast or Slow Stoneware Glaze Firing.

- **Drop:** 302°F (150°C) per hour to 1940°F (1060°C)
- **Hold:** 1.5 hours
- Cool naturally

Gold Luster Firing—Cone 018

Always refer to luster manufacturer instructions.

- **Ramp 1:** 392°F (200°C) per hour to 1274–1292°F (690–700°C)
- 15-minute soak
- Vents open throughout

Over Glaze Decals Firing—Cones 011–012

Always refer to decal manufacturer instructions.

- **Ramp 1:** 338°F (170°C) per hour to 788°F (420°C)
- **Ramp 2:** 392°F (200°C) per hour to 1616°F (880°C)
- 15-minute soak
- Vents open throughout

Pottery, Efficiency and the Environment

Pottery has an impact on the planet. Keeping accurate notes using this notebook for all your firings ensures your work will be more successful. Fewer dud pots means happier potters but also fewer refires and less waste. Here are some tips to maximize our efficiency and minimize our environmental impact.

- When buying a kiln, choose one with the thickest insulation; it will be more energy efficient.
- Firing a full kiln is more energy efficient than firing a half-empty kiln. Always fire your kilns full. Tumble stack your bisque. As the pottery is unglazed, work can touch and be stacked together in the kiln. Make sure you leave a little wiggle room so pieces don't crack each other. Glazed work cannot touch each other, or it will stick together!
- Ensure your work is fully dried before putting it in your kiln. This includes after glazing. I always wait 24 hours after glazing before loading my kiln.
- Excess moisture wears your elements quicker and as a result they use more energy (not to mention may cause explosions).
- Fast glaze firings are more energy efficient. When it comes to kiln schedules, it's a balancing act of using the most energy-efficient firing schedule possible while still getting your desired results. There are critical points of the firing where it's important to go slow, e.g., at the beginning and at the end. Start slow, speed it up and slow down again at the end.
- Your pots could be around for the next 1,000 years! Be discerning. Bad work equals landfill. Not every pot needs to be fired. Only chose your best work to fire. Reclaim the rest. Encourage your students to do the same.
- Clay and glazes are mined. Their production has an impact on the planet. Ask your pottery supplier where your clay and glaze materials come from. Ask if oxides are responsibly sourced. Choose clay sourced from within your country, if possible.

- Use a "three bucket glaze reclaim system." Rinse all your glazing tools in one bucket, then dip a second time in the next bucket. A dip in the third bucket should come out clean. Once the first bucket is full of glaze material, use this as a mystery glaze. Alternatively, evaporate all the water, fire it in a sacrificial pot and throw it away.
- Ensure your local energy is from 100% renewables. This is not the same as "backed by" 100% renewable energy.
- Vacuum your kiln every few firings. Dust and debris which inevitably build up over time will make the elements work harder.

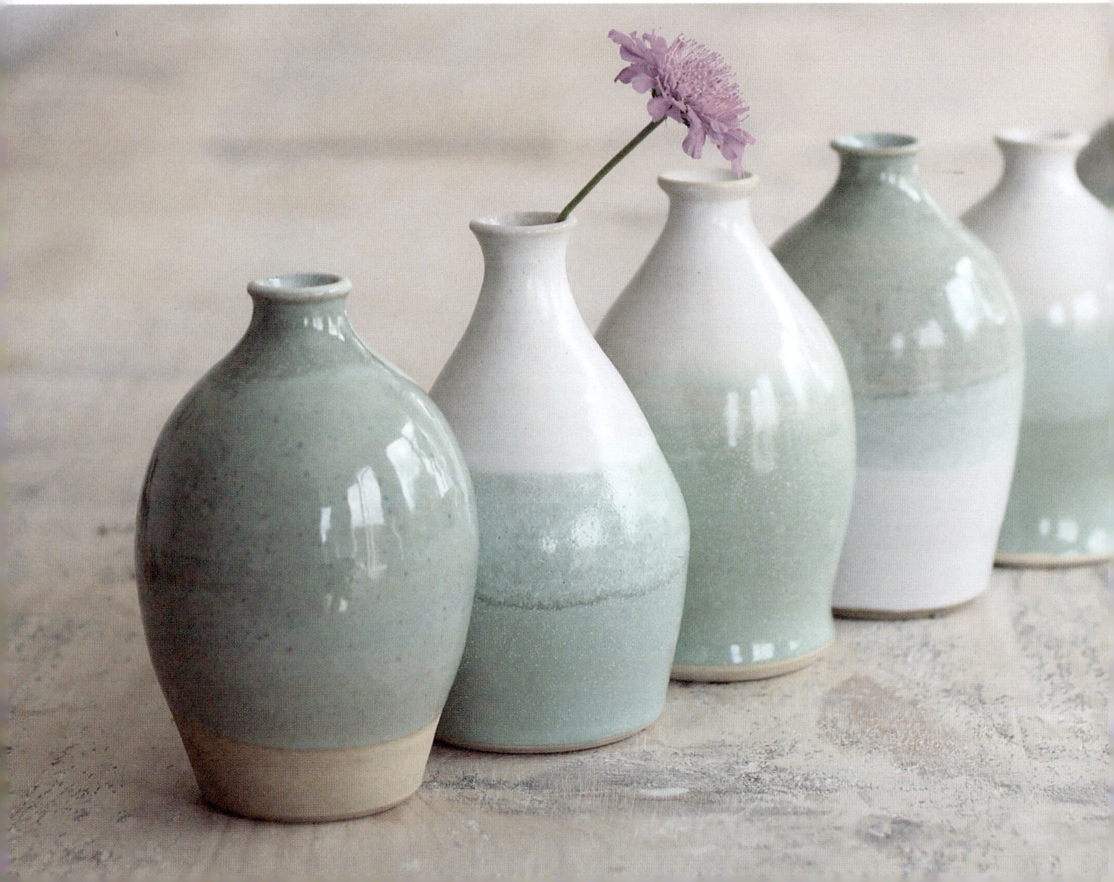

Acknowledgments

Thanks must go to Leela Chakravarti for the friendship and advice. Jodie Crooks Giles, who advised me on the environmental impact of kilns and firings. Tom Mcinnerney and Mary Trabue at The Edward Orton Foundation, for checking the accuracy of the content of this book and for generally cheering me on. And to my team at Page Street Publishing, especially my editor Alexandra Murphy and my designer Emma Hardy.

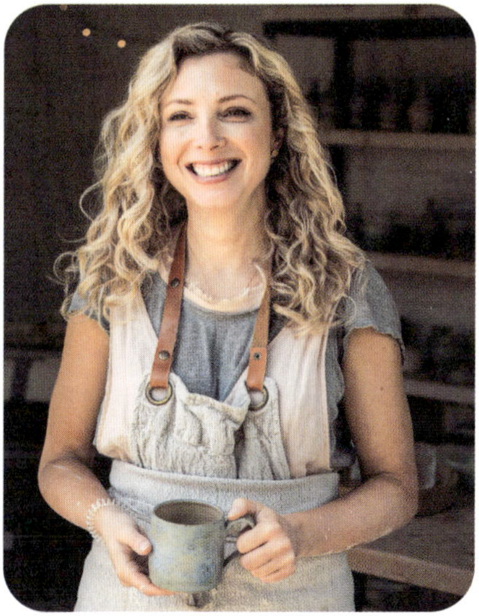

About the Author

Kara lives in a cottage in a tiny village just outside of Bath, U.K., with her husband, Tom, and two rescue kitties, Luna and Flora. You will often find her out in nature hiking or riding her horsey pal, Kizzy.

Kara's work is enjoyed by buyers all over the world. She designs and creates tableware for a Michelin-starred restaurant. Her work has been stocked in many shops and galleries including the prestigious Fortnum & Mason, London.

To learn more from Kara, join her Pottery Club community on Patreon, patreon.com/karaleighceramics, where she shares her passion for clay via detailed tutorial videos, projects, tips and tricks and heaps of pottery advice.

Follow Kara:

Instagram @karaleighceramics

YouTube @KaraLeighFordCeramics

TikTok @karaleighceramics

Threads @karaleighceramics